Yum-Yum Bento Box

Fresh Recipes for Adorable Lunches

By Crystal Watanabe
and Maki Ogawa

QUIRK BOOKS

PHILADELPHIA

Library of Congress Cataloging in Publication Number: 2009943046

ISBN: 978-1-59474-447-1

Printed in China

Typeset in Helvetica Rounded and Century Schoolbook

Designed by Jenny Kraemer
Production management by John J. McGurk

Photography by Maki Ogawa
Author photograph by Maki's son Kai Ogawa, who wants to be a cameraman when he grows up.

10 9 8 7 6 5 4

Quirk Books
215 Church Street
Philadelphia, PA 19106
www.quirkbooks.com

Visit www.yumyumbento.com!

Table of Contents

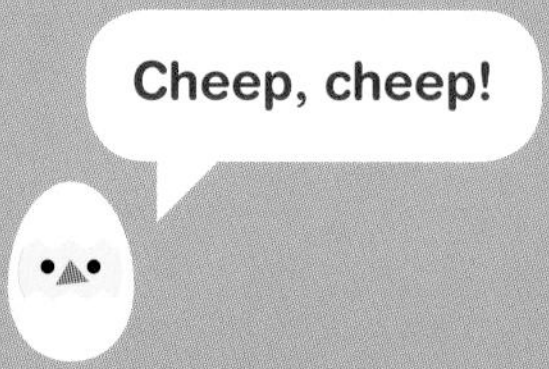
Cheep, cheep!

Hello, Obento!
An Introduction to
Japanese Lunches

Japanese boxed lunches are called *bento* (or, reverently, *obento*). These yummy, healthy meals are all the rage in Japan, where mothers think of them as an expression of love for their children. Bento boxes can be made from scratch, but they are also a great way to enjoy leftovers. Children and adults alike love to eat and make character-driven bento boxes, called *charaben* (or *kyaraben*). We hope you'll mix and match the recipes in this book to create your own tasty, portable meals. *Yum-Yum Bento Box* is a collection of some of our favorite lunches for our children and ourselves. They are almost too cute to eat!

According to a popular Japanese saying, it is important to "Eat with your eyes." This means more than just taking time to savor lovely, appetizing foods. Small, thoughtfully arranged dishes encourage portion control. And a rainbow of fruits, vegetables, fish, meats, rice, tofu, and cheeses central to the Japanese diet have given that country's population the highest longevity and lowest obesity rate in the world.

The bento tradition dates back centuries. As early as the 1500s Japanese farmers packed lunches to eat in the fields. In the late 1800s, Japanese immigrants moved to Hawaii to work in the sugarcane fields, and they brought the bento box tradition with them. These portable lunches have become a part of the island culture and are made at home and sold in take-out restaurants, supermarkets, and convenience stores. Just ask President Barack Obama, who grew up in Honolulu—he'll know exactly what a bento is. Today, online communities are an increasingly popular forum for sharing bento-making

■ Traditional bento

■ Charaben: character bento ■ Traditional bento

tips and techniques. It's a fun way to show our creations and learn new tricks. Like many mothers, we enjoy preparing simple, cute character bento boxes, called charaben or "deco ben" (because they are decorated bento). In this book, you'll find three types of character bentos: **Cuties & Critters**, modeled after pets and pals; **Fairy-Tale Friends**, inspired by magical stories; and **Special Day Treats**, perfect for celebrating big days or brightening up tough ones.

When my son started kindergarten, he cried and cried. I hoped that my bento would make him happy!   —Maki

Lovingly made bento boxes ease Japanese children into preschool by connecting school and the outside world with comforting foods from home. Mothers get up in the wee hours of the morning to prepare special obento for their children. At school, the finished creations are shared, compared, and even judged in cafeteria competitions. Online, bento makers share recipes and photos on Flickr, forums, and personal blogs. We gather inspiration from TV animation, old postage stamps, antiques, holidays, picture books, and our childrens' drawings. Bento is a fun, creative outlet, but another benefit can't be denied. Child obesity rates around the world continue to rise at an alarming rate, which leaves parents wondering: How do we get our children to eat healthier? How do we eat healthier? With its focus on smaller portions, adorable presentation, attractive color schemes, and tasty tidbits, bento is one answer to that question. We hope this book will provide you with fresh recipes, time-saving tricks, and helpful resources for your own adventures in bento making!

I found the online bento community and since I was starting Weight Watchers at the time, I decided to use bentos to regulate my portions. It worked! —Pikko

—Pikko & Maki

Packing a Bento Box

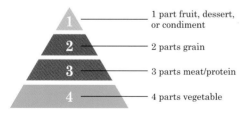

A good bento box packs in little tastes of everything—including occasional treats like bacon, cheese, and dessert. It's all about creatively presenting a fresh, well-balanced meal that's a delight to make and eat.

When assembling a bento box, aim for a 4:3:2:1 ratio of food groups.

- 1 — 1 part fruit, dessert, or condiment
- 2 — 2 parts grain
- 3 — 3 parts meat/protein
- 4 — 4 parts vegetable

Making your bento look full and attractive can be accomplished with a few simple additions. There's no recipe for beautiful garnishes: Use whatever fresh, colorful fruits and vegetables you have on hand to fill the gaps and add a pop of color to your bento. Green is easily added with broccoli, parsley, asparagus, and sugar snap peas. Red is easily added with whole or cut cherry tomatoes and strawberries. To save time, boil all your veggies together, removing them individually with a slotted spoon as soon as they are cooked.

Try to include colorful foods from every hue in the rainbow in each bento box. That will ensure a healthy balance of nutrients as well as a pretty presentation.

red · pink · orange
yellow · green · blue
violet · brown · black

Bento Boxes, Tools, and Accessories

A list of all available bento supplies would be endless, but there are a few key items and many inexpensive alternatives. For example, drinking straws and craft hole punches work just as well as most bento punches. Small hobby scissors are much more affordable than Fiskars micro-tip scissors. A toothpick can apply tiny whiskers to a kitty cat just as nicely as a special set of tweezers. And regular plastic storage containers can be used instead of fancy bento boxes.

■ A *donburi* bento box has two separate layers: one for holding rice and one for holding the food served on top of the rice. Under the top layer is a deep dish with lots of room for stew, rice, or chili.

■ Lacquer is used to coat both wood and plastic bento boxes. Wood is much heavier and longer lasting, but neither is microwave safe. Foods should be cooled before being placed into a lacquered bento box.

■ Most modern bento boxes are plastic. Affordable examples come in a rainbow of colors and themes, from panda bears to Hello Kitty.

(Note: Plastics numbered 3, 6, and 7 should be avoided for food use.) Remove the lid before microwaving.

■ In Japan, metal tins were traditionally reheated in an oven. Most schools today aren't equipped with ovens, so metal bento boxes and collectable or vintage cookie tins like these serve as a more eco-friendly option. When buying one, be sure it seals tightly.

■ *Onigiri* (rice ball) bento boxes are typically designed to fit 3 triangular onigiri boxes. A rounded triangular rooftop-like cover encloses the onigiri boxes, and underneath is a small container for side dishes.

■ In addition to the larger style are single-serving onigiri boxes, designed for one triangle onigiri. They can be carried around for a quick midmorning snack and fit in anything from a purse to a backpack.

■ Bamboo bento boxes look like covered baskets with slits in the sides that let air circulate, keeping sandwiches or rice balls from getting soggy. Line them with wax paper first.

■ To keep food hot or cold, use a thermal lunch jar by brands like Zojirushi or Tiger. They come with stacked containers that fit neatly into an insulating thermos.

■ The majority of bento boxes today are plastic, but traditional wooden bento boxes are still available online. These boxes are usually priced higher and require plastic lining to avoid staining. Do not microwave.

■ This traditional Asian utensil isn't just for eating sushi. Available in larger sizes, cooking chopsticks help scramble eggs, roll omelets, and tuck foods into bento boxes.

■ Children's bento boxes often have a matching set of utensils and a special case that matches the box.

■ Available as a set of three different pencils, each tip a different width, condiment pencils are a great way to draw with thick sauces such as ketchup, katsu sauce, or mayonnaise.

■ Wiener shapers transform hot dogs into cute crabs, tulips, octopi, and penguins. Not all cutters work with all types of hot dogs, and they should be coated with cooking spray before use to avoid meat sticking in the grooves.

■ The most common type of food divider is the familiar "sushi grass," or *baran* as it's called in Japan. Pastel versions are available, as are a variety of shapes, sizes, and designs. Use them to keep foods and flavors separated. Silicone dividers can be reused again and again.

■ Japanese manufacturers sell nori punches worldwide, but regular paper punches work just as well and can be found in almost any crafting or scrapbooking store.

■ Straws of all sizes make great food cutters for facial features such as eyes, nostrils, and cheeks. They can be bent into ovals, triangles, and petals or cut to make scalloped edges.

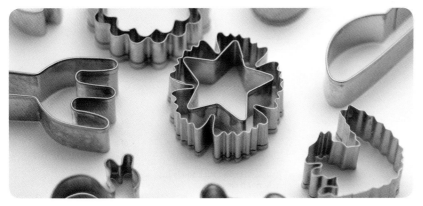

■ Although there are cutters specifically for vegetables, mini cookie cutters and fondant cutters can also be used for food. Themed sets are available. Metal cutters are great for slicing through thick pieces of raw vegetables, something that plastic cutters can't accomplish with the same efficiency.

■ A good, sharp knife is one of your best friends when making bento, but kitchen scissors can be a great time-saver for cutting leftover meat or shaping strips of nori. Just make sure they are dry before cutting nori.

■ Easy-to-use egg molds shape a still-warm egg into something much more fun and exciting, like a rabbit, star, fish, or car. Use sauces or food coloring to tint your creations. Molds are also available for tiny quail eggs.

■ Plastic cutters are best suited for soft foods such as meats, cheeses, and omelets. You can also buy charaben sets specifically made for bento making, or fondant-icing cutter sets which are more readily available.

■ Hand-held hole punches are great ways to make eyes out of sheets of nori. The standard and ⅛-inch sizes are great to have on hand. Be sure to label them for kitchen use only!

■ Little micro-tip scissors and tweezers help cut and arrange tiny nori smiley faces and other delicate foods.

■ Sushi mats are a useful tool for making *maki sushi* (sushi rolls) and shaping rolls of *tamagoyaki* into a nice rectangle shape. You can also use a sheet of aluminum foil; it's not as easy, but it does the trick!

■ Traditional onigiri shapes are easily made by hand (page 131), but onigiri molds are useful for complicated shapes like stars, hearts, bears, rabbits, and rolls. Wetting a mold before use will help the rice come out more easily.

■ Toothpicks are great for placing small nori pieces onto a rice ball, cutting cheese into shapes, or making a home-made flag. And they secure loose foods so that your bento stays in place when you take it to work or school.

■ Sandwich cutters come with one additional and vital piece: a matching design press. Shaped the same size as the cutter, the press will "etch" a design into your bread, making sandwiches even more adorable.

■ With its wide, flat surface, a rice paddle can form rice into a compact, flat surface much more efficiently than a large spoon or fork. Rice paddles are available in bamboo or plastic in a variety of sizes.

■ Bento boxes can be hard to find. Try testing out your ideas first using a simple plastic container. Bento is about presentation, and the box your lunch is in isn't necessarily the most important part of that.

■ Wax-coated paper cups are great for containing moist side dishes, such as pickled vegetables, and keeping foods separated. In a pinch, regular cupcake cups will also do the trick.

■ Plastic cups keep their shape and are the perfect holder for side dishes that contain liquid. Colorful and sometimes equipped with lids, they can be used as a central point for building your bento.

■ Silicone cups are usually for baking, but there are special ones made just for bento. They come in pastel colors and a variety of cute shapes. Mini silicone cups make great side containers for a bento.

■ Tracing paper is great for transferring patterns in this book, images of popular cartoons, or your own drawings and designs.

■ Plastic wrappers with cute designs add an additional layer of protection for your rice balls while making them look colorful and pretty.

■ These decorative picks— food picks, cupcake picks, cocktail sticks, and bento picks—are typically made of plastic, but fancier wooden types with painted designs are also available. Their benefits include their bright colors, cute designs, and reusability. Use them to secure foods or for eating the foods in the bento.

■ These little containers hold condiments such as ketchup, mayonnaise, and mustard. Although you can save condiments packets from restaurants, these versions add a nice touch to a bento's overall look.

■ These sauce bottles hold a single serving of various sauces or dressing like soy sauce or vinegar. They come in many different shapes and colors. Try to find a set that comes with a sauce plunger to fill the bottle.

■ Essentially a small, wet, reusable towel, the *oshibori* is used to wash hands before and after a meal. Packed in a small container separate from the lunch, it's a great way to freshen up.

■ Not all bento boxes have snap lids, and they may fall apart during transport. Some boxes come with straps that hold the lid or tiers together. Straps are also sold separately or can be made at home with elastic or fabric.

■ A traditional Japanese cloth wrapper, *furoshiki* is used to protect not just bento boxes but also gifts, clothes, and other goods.

It helps keep the layers of your box together. A *bento-bukuru* is a bag for bento; a bag fastened with string is a *kinchaku*.

■ A good plan is the best kitchen tool. Keeping a bento diary is an easy way to prepare healthy meals for the coming week. Brainstorm ways to incorporate dinner leftovers in the next day's bento. Artistic skills don't matter—it's all about having fun and being creative. Label each item for easy reference. Coloring bento sketches is not only fun; it also ensures a fresh, pretty arrangement and healthful balance of foods from every color of the rainbow.

Ingredients for Happy Faces

It's easy to eat a yummy, well-balanced meal when it's shaped like an adorable bunny rabbit or a roly-poly panda bear! Mix and match colorful ingredients to make happy faces—and even happier tummies.

Heads

rice ball head   hamburger bun head   hard-boiled egg head   omelet head

Eyes

nori eyes   cheese & nori eyes   crab & nori eyes   sesame seed eyelashes

Noses

pea nose   black-olive nose   cheese snout   deli meat snout

Mouths

  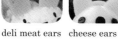

nori mouth   cheese & nori mouth   carrot beak   corn beak

Cheeks

rosy ketchup cheeks   deli meat cheeks   sausage (or radish) cheeks   carrot cheeks

Ears

deli meat ears   cheese ears   meatball ears   fried noodle antennae

Hair

spaghetti hair   fried egg hair   nori hair   cheese hair

Accessories

deli meat scarf   deli meat hood   cheese & herb hat pin   fried tofu hat

Rice Balls (*Onigiri*)

Rice balls can be flavored, colored, or shaped into a world of characters (*charaben*), from caterpillars to kitty cats. Compact and tidy, rice balls are easy to eat on the go.

Deli Meat

Thinner cuts are easier to wrap around rice or vegetables; thicker ones are easier to cut into shapes with a knife or cookie cutter.

Veggies

Corn kernels make cute noses, beaks, or flowers; lettuce keeps different foods separated; and broccoli and cherry tomatoes are a pretty way to fill up a bento box.

Hot Dogs

Slice hot dogs in half diagonally for a pretty finish. Or shape them into octopuses, crabs, or flowers. Picks make them easy finger food.

Condiments & Garnishes

Condiments glue on eyes and noses, and help attach other features. Spaghetti noodles and cupcake picks also work well. Cooked noodles can tie carrot sticks into portable bundles.

Nori

Paper-thin sheets of nori are made from sundried seaweed. It is low in carbohydrates and rich in minerals and vitamins B and C. Plus it's easy to cut with scissors or paper punches.

Cheese

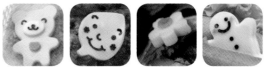

Calcium-rich cheeses can be cut into fun shapes. Tuck little packaged cheeses such as Babybel and Laughing Cow into boxed lunches.

Eggs

Peeled hard-boiled eggs can be cut into fun shapes, decorated, or tinted with food coloring. While hot, they can be molded into shapes. Quail eggs are small and dainty.

Sesame Seeds

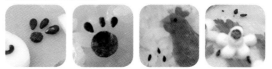

Teardrop-shape white or black sesame seeds make yummy eyelashes or other decorations.

Cuties & Critters

Some of our favorite lunchbox pals are everyday characters: adorable animals, cheerful friends, and happy sea creatures. You can mix and match these simple recipes to create your very own cuties and critters, using whatever ingredients you have on hand. Try tinting Kitty Cat with spices or food coloring to look like your family's pet. Give the Retro Girls yellow (cheddar cheese) hair to look like blonde friends. Or leave the Tiger Cubs white and make them into zebras! The possibilities are endless.

Baby Bear

 20 mins

One meatball sliced in half makes ears for Baby Bear!

You can make this little bear's head out of an oval *inarizushi*—rice stuffed into a tasty fried tofu pillow—or anything from a mini hamburger to a breakfast patty. Fill the box with crispy panfried fish, broccoli, a flower-cut egg, a cherry tomato skewered with a cupcake pick, or other bite-size snacks. A green pea makes a cute nose!

Baby Bear

- ½ fried tofu skin (store-bought or home-made, pages 134 to 135)
- about ½ cup rice (page 130)
- 2 lettuce leaves
- 1 small meatball
- 1 uncooked spaghetti noodle
- 1 or 2 cooked broccoli florets
- 1 green pea
- 1 piece nori

1. Stuff the tofu skin with rice and place into bento box. Line the rest of the box with lettuce leaves.

2. Slice the meatball in half and attach baby bear's ears by sticking little pieces of uncooked spaghetti through the meat and into the tofu-wrapped rice. Use broccoli to prop up the meatballs.

3. Use a drinking straw to punch a shallow hole in the center of the tofu-wrapped rice; nestle the green pea into it. Cut eyes and a smile out of nori with kitchen scissors.

Flower-Cut Egg

- 1 chicken or quail egg, hard-boiled and peeled

1. Cut off the top of the egg in a zigzag pattern for a flower-like edge. Use spinach or lettuce for pretty flower leaves.

Crispy Panfried Fish

- 1 fish fillet, such as halibut, flounder, or trout
- about 1 tbsp flour
- a few tbsp extra-virgin olive oil
- 1½ tsp soy sauce
- ½ tsp sake
- 1 tsp sugar
- ½ tsp mirin (or any cooking wine)
- about 2 tsp white sesame seeds

1. Cut the fish into 4 pieces and then dust with flour. Heat oil in a pan over medium heat. Sauté fish until crisp and golden, about 2 minutes on each side.

2. Combine soy sauce, sake, sugar, and mirin (or other seasonings) and pour into the pan with the fish. Sauté for 1 minute over low heat. Sprinkle with white sesame seeds before tucking pieces into the bento box.

Caterpillar

Give this hungry caterpillar some healthy snacks to munch on, such as sesame chicken nuggets, little flower eggs, simmered squash with mushrooms (page 136), one bright red cherry tomato, and a sweet slice of pear garnished with a mint leaf for dessert!

Caterpillar

- 2 lettuce leaves
- 4 small rice balls (page 131)
- 1 piece nori
- 1 uncooked spaghetti noodle
- a few tsp extra-virgin olive oil

1. Arrange lettuce and rice balls in a half circle in the bento box. Let the ruffled edge of the lettuce frame the caterpillar.

2. Arrange other foods in the bento box; then use a hole punch to make 11 dots out of nori for the caterpillar's eyes and spots.

3. Make rosy cheeks for the caterpillar by using a drinking straw to punch two circles out of the deli meat left over from the little flowers; attach by sticking little pieces of spaghetti through them and into the rice ball.

4. Fry uncooked spaghetti noodle in olive oil until golden brown and crispy. Snap off two small pieces to make the antennae.

Make caterpillar antennae with a piece of crispy fried spaghetti!

Sesame Chicken Nuggets

- 4 or 5 bite-size pieces chicken breast
- 1 tsp salt
- 1 tbsp cornstarch
- ½ tsp black sesame seeds
- ¼ tsp curry powder
- a few tbsp oil for frying

1. In a bowl, marinate chicken in ¼ cup water and salt for 20 minutes.

2. Drain the water. Combine cornstarch, sesame seeds, and curry powder in a bowl. Coat chicken well. Heat oil in a pan over medium heat. Fry 5 minutes or until thoroughly cooked.

Little Flowers

- 1 piece fish sausage, or thick-sliced deli meat or cheese
- 1 chicken egg or 2 quail eggs, hard-boiled and peeled
- leftover fried spaghetti noodle from caterpillar

1. Use a flower-shape mini cutter to make flowers out of fish sausage, meat, or cheese.

2. Attach to the eggs by sticking small pieces of fried spaghetti through the center of each flower and into the egg.

Chickens

Small pieces of uncooked spaghetti noodle fasten the pink combs. In a few hours, moisture from the rice will make the noodles soft and edible!

Cluck, cluck! There's no poultry in this chicken bento box, only adorable chick-shape rice balls. Sautéed shrimp tastes great with steamed broccoli, a hot dog cut diagonally into three pieces, and bite-size pear slices skewered with a food pick.

Chickens

- 1 or 2 lettuce leaves
- 2 rice balls (page 131)
- 4 kernels frozen corn
- 1 slice pink fish sausage or deli meat
- 1 uncooked spaghetti noodle
- 1 piece nori, or 1 black olive

1. Line a bento box with lettuce. Arrange the rice balls, checking that they are framed by the lettuce's ruffled edge. Make an indentation in the middle of each one with a chopstick. Press in two pieces of corn, making beaks.

2. Cut sausage for cheeks and combs. Use ½-inch pieces of spaghetti noodle to attach combs to the rice.

3. Use a hole punch to make eyes out of nori paper (or cut circles out of a black olive).

Sautéed Shrimp with Mushrooms

- 3 shrimp, cleaned and deveined
- 2 tbsp plus ½ tsp sake, divided
- pinch of salt
- 1 tbsp cornstarch
- about 2 tbsp extra-virgin olive oil
- about 5 mushrooms, such as shimeji
- 1½ tsp ketchup
- pinch of salt and pepper
- 1 tsp minced leeks

1. In a small dish, marinate shrimp in 2 tbsp sake and salt for 5 minutes. Remove; blot moisture with a paper towel, and then sprinkle with cornstarch.

2. Warm oil in a pan over medium-high heat. Sauté mushrooms until tender; add shrimp and stir until almost cooked through. Mix in ½ tsp sake, ketchup, salt, pepper, and leeks. Let cool before spooning into the bento box.

It's easy to make a rolled-up omelet into little chicks with cooked-carrot beaks and food-pick feathers! See page 136 for how to do it.

You can boil a few pieces of broccoli and the hot dog at the same time. Use a slotted spoon to remove the hot dog after 1 minute, letting the broccoli boil another 2 minutes or just until tender.

Eek! A Mouse!

To make a white mouse, use a slice of white cheese. It'll melt into the mac and cheese when reheated at lunchtime.

Hungry mice love to nibble cheese! Fill half a bento box with a cup of yummy green pea mac & cheese (page 133). Then arrange garlic asparagus, two or three broccoli or cauliflower florets, and a cup of sautéed basil tomatoes. For dessert, slice 1 strawberry up to the stem (not cutting all the way through) and wrap it with a food divider or mini cupcake cup.

Pink Mouse

- 1 slice ham or bologna
- 1 piece nori

1. Trace circles below or use circle food cutters to make the mouse's head and ears out of sliced meat.

2. Use a hole punch to cut 3 dots out of nori for the eyes and nose. Cut out whiskers with scissors and apply. Put pink mouse into the bento box once everything else has been arranged.

❀ You can also use a nori punch to make a cute mousy smile!

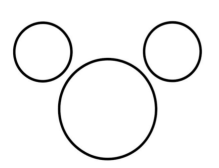

Sautéed Basil Tomatoes

- about 1 tsp extra-virgin olive oil
- 1 tsp minced onions
- a pinch garlic salt, to taste
- 3 to 5 cherry tomatoes
- 1 chopped basil leaf

1. Heat oil in a pan on medium-high heat. Add minced onions and sauté 1 or 2 minutes. Season with garlic salt.

2. Stir in tomatoes, tossing and cooking until skin starts to loosen. Add basil and cook until soft. Remove and let cool. Place a food cup into the bento box and fill it with the sautéed tomatoes.

Garlic Asparagus

- 2 asparagus stalks
- 1 tsp extra-virgin olive oil
- pinch of garlic salt

1. Peel bottoms of asparagus stalks. Heat olive oil in a pan over medium heat. Add asparagus and sprinkle with garlic salt. Continue cooking 3 minutes or until just tender.

2. Let cool and then arrange neatly next to other fruits and veggies.

Quail eggs make extra-tiny lambykins!

This little lamb's fleece can be white as snow—or pretty in pink! If you'd like to tint the egg, peel it and soak in food coloring or *memmi* sauce, a soy-sauce-based dipping sauce. Sprinkle Fluffy Lamb with salt as a snack or pack into a bento box with carrot and celery sticks and a cupcake cup filled with fresh fruits.

Fluffy Lamb

- ½ to 1 cup pink cooked rice (page 130)
- 1 chicken or quail egg, hard-boiled and peeled
- 2 dabs ketchup
- 1 piece nori
- 1 slice cheese

1. Scoop rice into a small cup or container. Nestle egg in the center.

2. Use a punch or scissors to cut a nose and eyes out of nori. Slice two ears out of cheese. Use a toothpick to dab on rosy ketchup cheeks.

❀ To slice a lamb ear out of cheese you can make two cuts with one drinking straw.

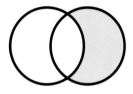

To make a white lamb, leave the rice untinted and dye the egg with food coloring or memmi sauce.

Frogs

A bear rice mold doubles as a frog mold. Or you can shape these rice-ball froggies with your hands.

Two frog friends ribbit together, bringing a smile to all who see them. Pack them with a colorfully balanced meal: three little pork patties, sesame spinach, a wedge of corn-on-the-cob, and a cherry tomato skewered with a cupcake pick.

Frog Friends

- a few lettuce leaves
- 2 green rice balls (pages 130 and 131)
- 1 slice white cheese
- 1 piece nori

1. Line a bento box with lettuce leaves and then place the two frogs in the box.

2. Use a fat drinking straw to cut out four cheese circles for the eyes. Top with four ovals cut or punched out of nori. Cut two smiles and four tiny dots out of nori (two for each frog's snout).

Pork Patties

- ¼ lb ground pork
- 1 tbsp oyster sauce
- ½ tsp salt
- ½ tsp pepper
- pinch scallions, chopped
- 1 tbsp extra-virgin olive oil

1. Mix the pork, oyster sauce, salt, pepper, and scallions together and form three small patties.

2. Warm oil in a pan over medium heat. Cook patties 10 minutes or until cooked through and slightly browned. Refrigerate to cool completely before arranging in the bento box.

Sesame Spinach

- 1 large handful spinach leaves
- pinch of salt
- ½ tsp grated garlic
- ½ tsp sesame oil
- pinch of white sesame seeds

1. Boil the leaves a few minutes or until tender. Drain well. Season with salt, garlic, sesame oil, and sesame seeds.

2. Put cooked greens into a small food cup in the bento box. Top with musical notes cut from carrots if desired.

❁ Replace spinach with choy sum leaves for sesame choy sum! Choy sum is a delicate and nutritious green.

You can use a musical-note food cutter to transform a slice of cooked carrot into a frog song. Save time by boiling the carrots and corn together.

Guardian Angel

15 mins

Punch a piece of cheese 3 times with the same circle cutter to make two football-shape pieces for the angel's bangs.

Alphabet-themed bentos can be a great way to teach children their letters. Suggestions for A foods: apple, asparagus, angel hair pasta, avocado, apricots. Decoration ideas starting with A: angels, autumn, animals, apes.

This little guardian angel will watch over your sandwich until lunchtime. Use a bird or angel cookie cutter to make her out of sliced cheese and deli meat. Cookie cutter shapes are easy to adapt: You can use a bird's wing and a gingerbread man's legs and cut out the rest by hand. Use mini alphabet cutters to make words out of scraps.

Angel

- 1 slice cheddar cheese
- ½ slice white cheese
- ¼ slice bologna, turkey, or ham
- 1 piece nori

1. Use a knife to cut the angel's dress out of cheddar cheese, and use an angel or bird cookie cutter to punch an angel wing out of white cheese. Trim to fit your angel.

2. With a knife or pink food cutter wheel, cut four curved limbs out of meat. Punch two mini circles: one meat and one cheddar cheese for the face and hair. Use same circle cutter to punch out two portions of the cheese circle for the angel's bangs; make her a cheese ponytail from the scraps. Use a smiley-face punch to make her features out of nori. Cut out the word ANGEL from the remaining cheese.

3. Place atop the sandwich once all other foods have been arranged and the bento is ready to go.

Creamy veggie dip fits neatly in a cute, reusable sauce container.

Peanut Butter & Apple Sandwich

- 2 to 4 slices bread
- a few tbsp peanut butter
- 1 apple, thinly sliced

1. Cut the sandwich bread to fit your bento box. Spread peanut butter on bread. Neatly layer apple slices onto one half and cover with the other slice of bread.

Snacks

- about ¼ cup crackers
- about ¼ cup dried apricots
- 1 carrot, peeled
- 1 celery stalk
- 1 individually packaged cheese wedge, such as Laughing Cow

1. Add a food cup next to the sandwich and fill it with crackers.

2. Slice dried apricots into strips. Arrange them in plastic food cup in a separate bento box.

3. Cut carrot and celery in half and trim to fit your bento box. Cut into eighths for mini carrot and celery sticks. Stack them next to the apricots, separated with the cheese wedge.

Hawaii Sun

This light and yummy dessert is called *haupia* (how-pee-ah) and commonly served at Hawaiian luaus and other gatherings.

A happy shining sun basks in the warmth of three yummy snacks popular in paradise! First made in Hilo, Hawaii, loco moco is an affordable, filling comfort food. Try topping it with soy sauce, ketchup, or hot sauce.

Sunny Loco Moco

- about 1 cup rice (page 130)
- 1 small hamburger patty
- 2 to 3 tbsp gravy
- 1 egg
- 1 piece nori

1. Put rice into the thermal jar, filling to about 1-inch from the fill line.

2. Fry hamburger patty until cooked through. Place onto the rice and pour gravy overtop.

3. Fry the egg sunny side up. Place it on top of the hamburger patty. Punch a smiley face out of nori; gently arrange the pieces onto the yolk to make a happy sun.

❀ Pack a bottle of soy sauce or other condiments if desired.

Try packing these easy-to-make Hawaiian dishes in a set of thermal lunch jars, which are great for keeping the main dish warm and the side dishes cool.

Salmon Tomato Salad

- ½ salted salmon fillet
- ¼ cup fresh tomato, chopped
- 2 tbsp onion, diced
- 1 tbsp green onions, chopped
- a sprig of parsley

1. Dice the salmon. Mix in tomato and onions and then scoop the mixture into a container. Top with parsley.

Coconut Pudding

- 4 to 6 tbsp sugar
- 4 to 6 tbsp cornstarch
- 1 (12-oz) can coconut milk
- a few raspberries or other fruit

1. Combine sugar and cornstarch and stir in 1½ cups water. Pour coconut milk into a saucepan over medium heat. Add the sugar mixture, cooking and stirring constantly until thickened.

2. Spoon into container or pour into a square pan and chill until firm (like Jell-O). Top with fruit.

Hungry Fishy

Crumbly seasoned meat, fish, or eggs are a bento staple called *soboro*. This tasty soboro-style ground beef is seasoned with soy sauce, sake, mirin, and sugar; you can try ground chicken or pork instead, or substitute the soy sauce, sugar, and sake with salt and pepper.

Scrambled eggs and seasoned ground beef can be made into fishies and other shapes by using sandwich or cookie cutters. Try making a broccoli bouquet (page 73) and a pretty red flower with a green leaf: Skewer a cherry tomato with a cupcake pick and arrange it next to a green bean cut in half on the diagonal.

Hungry Fishy

- about 1 cup rice (page 130)
- 1 egg, beaten
- 2 tsp extra-virgin olive oil
- ¼ cup ground beef
- 1 tsp soy sauce
- ½ tsp sake
- 1 tsp mirin, optional
- 1 tsp sugar
- about ¼ cup frozen peas and corn
- 1 asparagus stalk
- 1 green bean or snap pea
- 1 or 2 broccoli florets
- pinch of salt

1. Use a food divider and fill half the bento box with a flattened layer of rice. Put a fish-shape cutter on top of the rice [a].

2. Scramble egg over medium heat 4 minutes, using chopsticks to break it into extra-small pieces; set aside.

3. For soboro-style beef: Heat oil in a pan, add ground beef and stir until browned; mix in soy sauce, sake, mirin, and sugar. Simmer until most of the liquid is gone. Spoon beef inside [b] and scrambled egg outside of the fish-shape cutter. Gently remove it.

4. Boil all veggies with a pinch of salt. Use a slotted spoon to remove the peas and corn after 30 seconds, the asparagus and green bean after 1 minute, and the broccoli after 2 minutes. Arrange broccoli and asparagus next to the hungry fishy. One green pea makes an eye [c]. Fill the rest of the box with veggies, a condiment case of mayo or veggie dip, and wrapped candies or other treats [d].

Kitty Cat & Goldfish

30 mins

Make Kitty's nose with the cap of a small mushroom or the tip of an olive!

What makes this white cat so happy? A yummy goldfish made out of a carrot! Plus some stir fry (page 41) and a few bite-size pieces of simmered squash (page 136) or other snacks. Just make sure that a lettuce leaf or food divider separates Kitty Cat from other foods.

Kitty Cat

- pinch of salt
- ½ cup rice (page 130)
- 1 lettuce leaf
- 1 piece nori
- 1 small mushroom cap, left over from stir fry
- 3 slices carrot

1. Sprinkle salt over the rice. Shape it into an oval with two triangular ears. Put it into the bento box, using lettuce to separate it from other food. Cut whiskers, eyes, and mouth out of nori using kitchen scissors.

2. Make the nose with the cap of a brown mushroom or the end of an olive. Use two thin carrot slices for cheeks and a thicker one for the fish.

❀ Use a paring knife to cut a slice of carrot into a goldfish. Cooked carrots are easier to cut than uncooked carrots, but both are tasty.

❀ You can cut cat-eye (or football) shapes by cutting the same thing twice with a drinking straw or circle cutter.

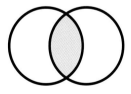

You can make black cats by wrapping rice balls with nori and adding eyes made out of cheddar cheese.

Miss Octopus

If you don't like bologna, try cutting Miss Octopus out of cheese instead! Or make mini hot-dog octopuses.

Pretty Miss Octopus loves broccoli, Japanese-style fried chicken (page 133), protein-packed potato and tuna salad, and cherry tomatoes skewered with cupcake picks.

Miss Octopus

- 1 slice bologna
- 1 piece white cheese
- 1 piece nori
- a few lettuce leaves
- 1 blue rice ball (pages 130 to 131)

1. Trace shapes or use a food cutter wheel to make a circle and eight legs out of bologna. Add two eyes punched out of cheese with a wide drinking straw.

2. Cut a nose, smile, and eyelashes out of nori and apply them to Miss Octopus's face.

3. Line the bento box with lettuce. Lightly salt and wet your hands, and then flatten the blue rice into a round, flat shape. Put it into the bento box. Arrange Miss Octopus on top after other foods have been added.

Potato & Tuna Salad
Makes about 4 servings, enough for leftovers

- 1 potato, boiled
- ½ can tuna fish
- 2 tbsp mayo
- ¼ cup diced onion
- ¼ cup diced celery
- pinch of salt and pepper

1. Peel the potato and chop it into bite-size cubes.

2. In a bowl, flake the tuna fish so that the pieces are small. Mix in potatoes, mayo, onion, celery, salt, and pepper. Scoop salad into a plastic food cup or use a lettuce leaf to separate it from other foods in your bento box.

How to Make a Hot-Dog Octopus

❶ Using a knife, cut a mini hot dog or cocktail wiener in half diagonally.

❷ Slice legs into the bottom. (There isn't always room for eight; four or five will do!)

❸ Boil about 30 seconds, and the legs will unfurl!

❹ Add eyes made of cheese, nori, or Letter O noodles from alphabet soup.

Serve little piggy burgers with fresh fruit and juice boxes, or pack them into bento boxes with other tasty snacks (pages 134 to 136).

Two Piggy Burgers

- 2 slices white cheese
- 2 mini hamburger buns
- 2 small hamburger patties, grilled
- 1 or 2 lettuce leaves
- 2 slices tomato
- 1 slice ham or salami
- 1 piece nori
- a pat of butter

1. Use a cookie cutter to cut the cheese into a pretty shape. Toast buns. Sandwich the burgers with lettuce, tomato, and cheese. Secure with picks.

2. Make 2 pig snouts plus 2 ovals out of ham. Cut ovals in half to make ears. Cut eyes and smiles out of nori or the leftover cheese. Melt butter in the microwave; brush it over the tops of the buns to make it easy to stick on the snouts, ears, and nori smiley faces.

How to Make a Pig Snout

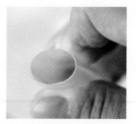

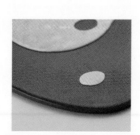

❶ Gather a few drinking straws of varying widths.

❷ Pinch a fat straw so that the end is an oval.

❸ Punch an oval out of a piece of lunchmeat, cheese, or other thin food.

❹ Punch two snout holes using a thinner straw. Oink, oink!

How to Make Food Picks

❶ All you need is patterned tape, toothpicks, and scissors.

❷ Lay a toothpick on top of the sticky side of the tape.

❸ Fold the tape over onto itself, and then trim it to make a little flag.

❹ Done! Stick your pretty picks into piggy burgers or other foods.

Polar Bear

Make a polar bear nose out of a small mushroom or the tip of a black olive!

When they come out of hibernation, polar bears hunt across the Arctic in search of nutritious food. But this lucky polar bear won't have to look far: It's warm and cozy in a box full of veggie-and-pork stir fry, steamed broccoli, and cherry tomatoes skewered with food picks.

Polar Bear

- ½ cup rice (page 130)
- 1 lettuce leaf
- 1 piece nori
- 1 small mushroom, left over from the stir fry, or the tip of a black olive
- a few dabs of ketchup
- 6 black sesame seeds

1. Add a pinch of salt to the rice and shape it into a bear-shape rice ball with your hands or a bear-shape mold. Place it in the bento box, propping it up with stir fry or other foods and framing it with lettuce.

2. Cut two round eyes and a smile out of nori. Use a small mushroom or the tip of an olive for the nose. Dab on rosy ketchup cheeks with a toothpick. Add black sesame seed eyelashes.

Paw Print

- 1 egg, hard-boiled and peeled
- 1 piece nori
- a dab of mayo

1. Gently cut off the top half of the egg white, leaving the yolk intact. Use kitchen scissors to cut one big circle and three small circles out of nori; Use a dab of mayo to stick a paw print onto the yolk. Add egg to the bento box once other foods have been arranged.

Veggie-and-Pork Stir Fry

- 1 or 2 tbsp extra-virgin olive oil
- 2 slices eggplant, cut into bite-size pieces
- 8 to 10 mushrooms, such as shimeji
- ½ oz ground pork
- 1 tsp soy sauce
- 2 or 3 edamame pods or green beans
- 2 steamed broccoli florets or other veggies

1. Heat oil in a pan and stir fry eggplant, mushrooms, and pork for a few minutes. Sprinkle with soy sauce and edamame or green beans. Save one mushroom cap for the polar bear's nose.

2. Scoop stir fry into the bento box, using broccoli to separate it from the polar bear.

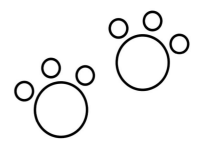

Trace this template to make paw prints!

Retro Girls

Cut retro girls' hair out of nori paper or a slice of roast beef (brunette) or cheddar cheese (blonde)!

You a

Cute retro girls love their bob haircuts, jukebox music, and yummy potato dumplings (page 79)! Ham and carrots left over from their cheeks and noses can be diced and rolled into a finger-food omelet (page 136).

Retro Girls

- 1 piece nori
- 2 rice balls (page 131), flattened
- 8 black sesame seeds
- 2 asparagus stalks, cut in half
- 2 thinly sliced baby carrots
- 1 slice ham
- 1 cherry tomato

1. Cut two ½-inch-wide strips of nori. Wrap each rice ball with a strip while rice is hot. A dab of water will secure the ends. Cut leftover nori into bob haircuts, eyes, and smiles; add them to the rice balls once the rice has cooled. Use sesame seeds for eyelashes.

2. Boil asparagus and sliced carrot; use a slotted spoon to remove the asparagus after 1 minute and the carrot after 4 minutes. Use a drinking straw to cut two noses out of carrot slices. Use a wider straw to cut ham for their cheeks.

3. Line the bento box with lettuce leaves; add the retro girls, making sure the ruffled edge of the lettuce frames their faces. Apply their noses and cheeks. Tuck in the asparagus and skewered cherry tomato.

How to Make Your Own Bento Patterns

❶ Lay tracing paper over a drawing and trace it in pencil. Trim the edges ¼ inch from the edge.

❷ Place pattern atop a piece of nori paper (or sliced cheese, deli meat, or other thin foods).

❸ Use kitchen scissors to cut the pattern from the food. Done!

Sandwich Cuties

Cut off the ends of baby carrots and then quarter them into little carrot sticks.

Any sandwich can be made into cute bite-size sandwiches! Try fillings like peanut butter and jelly, ham and cheese, turkey, bologna, or roast beef. Lettuce stays fresh all day because it doesn't touch the sandwich condiments; it can be ripped into pieces and tucked into the sandwiches at lunchtime.

Mini Ham & Cheese Sandwiches

- 2 lettuce leaves
- 2 slices bread
- 2 slices ham and cheese or other fillings
- mayo or other condiments

1. Line the bento box with lettuce leaves.

2. Use mini sandwich bento punches or animal-shape cookie cutters to make cute shapes out of the bread and fillings.

3. Spread condiments on the bread. Assemble mini sandwiches and arrange them in the bento box alongside fruits and veggies.

How to Make a Checkered Apple

Checkered or checkerboard apples are a cute bento tradition. They can be made in about 5 minutes with nothing more than a fresh apple and a good paring knife.

❶ Quarter an apple with a sharp paring knife. Take one slice, remove the core, and trim the bottom for a flat, square shape.

❷ Score a grid into the apple skin. (Larger grids are easier because you don't have to cut out as many squares.)

❸ Slide the tip of the knife underneath the skin of every other square, popping out a square of apple skin.

❹ Done! Briefly soak your checkered apple in lemon water (or lightly salted water) to prevent browning.

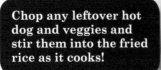

Chop any leftover hot dog and veggies and stir them into the fried rice as it cooks!

The sun is smiling! Have a happy lunchtime with crunchy croquettes (page 121), hot-dog crabs, cherry tomatoes, sliced peaches, and a pretty pink cupcake for dessert (page 137).

Sunshine Corn
Makes about 6 servings, enough for leftovers

- 1 ear of corn, boiled and cut into rounds
- 1 slice provolone cheese
- dab of mayo
- 1 piece nori

1. Refrigerate or freeze extra rounds of corn for later use. With a toothpick or cookie cutter, punch a circle out of cheese. Stick it onto the corn with mayo.

2. Use a smiley-face punch or kitchen scissors to cut eyes, nose, and a smile out of nori; put them onto the sun once all other foods have been arranged in the bento box.

Hot-Dog Crab

- 1 hot dog
- 1 tbsp soy sauce
- 1 tbsp sugar
- 1 serving fried rice (page 132) or pasta

1. Trim hot dog to the length of the crab cutter and slice in half lengthwise. Use the cutter to create a crab shape.

2. Heat soy sauce, sugar, and 1 tbsp water in a saucepan over medium heat. Stir until sugar is dissolved; lower heat. Add hot-dog crab and simmer until the legs and eyes perk up. Fill half a bento box with fried rice. Top with two hot-dog crabs.

How to Make a Hot-Dog Crab

Crab cutters are a quick and easy way to gussy up hot dogs. If you don't have this tool, you can use a kitchen knife to make hot dogs into crabs, octopuses (page 37), or flowers (page 65).

❶ Spray a hot dog crab cutter lightly with cooking spray.

❷ Insert a mini hot dog or cocktail wiener into the cutter. Place the cap on top and push down, but not all the way.

❸ Flip the cutter over and remove the hot-dog crab. Use a knife to finish the leg cuts. Done!

❹ Boiling in water or simmering in seasonings perks up cut hot dog critters.

Teddy Bear Grilled Cheese

🕐 | **15 mins**

These cheesy teddy bears have hearts made out of ham. Decorate sandwiches with cheese shaped with any mini cookie cutter!

This classic sandwich bento box is packed with grilled-cheese teddy bears, apple bunnies, and other simple childhood favorites. Kids will love assembling the ants on a log at lunchtime.

Teddy Bear Grilled Cheese

- 2 pats butter
- 2 slices bread
- 2 slices cheddar cheese, 1 slice white cheese
- 1 piece nori
- 1 small piece of ham

1. Melt butter in a pan over medium heat. Cut crusts off bread. Place bread into the pan and grill until golden brown, flipping once.

2. Sandwich one slice of cheese between the warm, toasty bread. Set aside to cool. Cut sandwich in half and put it into the bento box, stacking the halves to fit.

3. Cut teddy bears from the other slice of cheese and add ovals cut out of white (or cheddar) cheese to make teddy bear faces. Decorate the sandwich, adding nori smiley faces and tiny ham-shape hearts.

Ants on a Log

- 2 celery stalks, cut into sticks
- peanut butter
- raisins

1. Arrange celery sticks in the bento box. Spoon peanut butter into a food cup. Use individually boxed raisins or put a few into a mini food cup.

How to Make an Apple Bunny

Like checkered apples (page 45), apple bunnies are a cute bento tradition. They can be made in about 5 minutes with nothing but a fresh apple and a good paring knife.

❶ Quarter an apple with a paring knife. Take one slice, remove the core, and trim one end square and one end pointy.

❷ Starting at the square end, slide the knife under the apple skin, peeling it about halfway.

❸ Cut out a triangle of the apple skin to make the V shape. Curl up the bunnies' ears between your thumb and the knife.

❹ Briefly soak your Apple Bunny in iced lemon water: cold water will help curl the ears, and lemon will preserve color.

Tiger Cubs

20 mins

Boiling sliced carrot for 1 minute makes it easier to cut, and you can save time by adding a few broccoli florets or other veggies to the pot.

Don't want to use ketchup to color your rice? Mix in finely grated carrot!

Rawr!! Hungry baby tigers need lots of yummy meat and veggies, such as these easy-to-nibble rolled-up omelets (page 136), corned beef hash patties, green beans & SPAM, broccoli, skewered cherry tomatoes, and carrot flowers.

Tiger Cubs

- 1 to 2 tbsp ketchup
- about 1 cup rice (page 130)
- 2 or 3 lettuce leaves
- 1 piece nori
- 4 black sesame seeds

1. Mix ketchup into the rice until it is an even orange color. Use your hands or a bear-shape rice-ball mold to form two flat, tiger-shape rice balls.

2. Line the bento box with lettuce leaves. Prop up the tigers with other foods. Fold nori 3 times and cut 6 sets of triangles for the stripes. Use a punch or scissors to cut out noses, smiles, and eyes. Add sesame seed eyelashes to the girl cub.

Green Beans & SPAM
Makes about 6 servings, enough for leftovers

- 1 can SPAM
- 2 cups fresh green beans
- 1 tbsp extra-virgin olive oil
- 1 tbsp soy sauce
- 1 tsp pepper

1. Thinly slice SPAM and green beans. Warm oil in a pan over medium-high heat. Fry SPAM until it begins to turn reddish brown; add the green beans.

2. Continue frying until the beans become bright green and tender. Season with the soy sauce and pepper, and cook 2 more minutes.

❀ SPAM gets a bad rap. But when thinly sliced and panfried, it is delicious and actually healthier than most processed foods. It's a quick way to boost protein and flavor in veggie dishes.

Corned Beef Hash Patties
Makes about 8 servings, enough for leftovers

- several tbsp extra-virgin olive oil
- 1 onion, chopped
- 1 (12-oz) can corned beef
- 2 boiled potatoes
- 1 carrot, grated or finely chopped
- 1 egg
- 1 tsp salt and a pinch of pepper
- panko or bread crumbs, as needed

1. Heat oil in a pan over medium heat. Sauté the onion 2 minutes; add the corned beef and fry until the meat has separated nicely.

2. In a separate bowl, mash the potatoes. Add the corned beef, onions, carrot, egg, salt, and pepper, mixing well. Chill in fridge until firm. If the mixture is still too soft, add some bread crumbs or panko. Form into patties and fry in olive oil until browned on both sides.

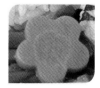

You can use a mini cutter to make carrot flowers.

Walruses

🕐 | **30 mins**

I can haz walrus bento?

Everybody knows that walruses love to munch tasty veggie tempura! Green beans, broccoli, chopped herbs, squash, or other mixed veggies can be used in this adaptable tempura recipe. Fill the rest of the bento box with turkey-wrapped green beans, a few steamed broccoli florets, and a bright red cherry tomato wedge.

Walruses

- 2 brown rice balls and 2 small brown rice ovals (pages 130 to 131)
- 2 lettuce leaves
- 1 piece nori
- 2 mushroom caps, or lentils
- a few dabs of ketchup
- 1 piece white cheese

1. Place the two large rice balls into the bento box on top of lettuce leaves. Gently press rice ovals into the walrus faces. Cut tiny circles out of nori to make the walrus's whiskers.

2. Use mushroom caps (left over from the veggie tempura) for noses. Use a toothpick to dab on ketchup cheeks; then add four white-cheese walrus tusks.

❀ Use a toothpick to cut little walrus tusks out of sliced cheese.

Veggie Tempura

- 1 tbsp flour
- 3 or 4 bite-size cubes of pumpkin or squash
- 3 or 4 mushrooms, such as shimeji or maitake
- 2 green beans
- 1 or 2 sprigs fresh parsley, chopped
- several tbsp extra-virgin olive oil

1. To make tempura batter, put flour in a bowl with ½ tbsp ice water; stir. Toss squash, mushrooms, beans, and parsley with the batter. Deep fry in olive oil over medium heat.

Turkey-Wrapped Green Beans

- 3 green beans
- 1 slice turkey
- a few tsp extra-virgin olive oil

1. Wrap green beans in turkey. Cut in half to make 2 rolls and secure the ends with toothpicks.

2. Warm oil in a pan. Quickly sear turkey-wrapped green beans over medium-high heat to seal the meat around the green beans in a crisp, tidy roll. Cut in half and remove toothpicks before tucking turkey-wrapped green beans into the bento box.

Fairy-Tale Friends

Re-create characters from your favorite fairy tales and magical stories! Little Red Riding Hood, Alice in Wonderland, Snow White, and Matroyshka (better known as Russian Nesting Dolls) are so beloved by bento makers that custom fairy-tale bento boxes and accessories are becoming widely available (see Shopping Guide, pages 139 to 140). You can also use the techniques in this chapter to make cute bento versions of popular cartoon characters and storybook heroes.

Enchanted Forest Friends

Cute critters can be made out of a flat omelet with mini food cutters. Grilled SPAM is much used in Hawaii, and these petite versions of the traditional SPAM *musubi* (wrapped with rice balls) are not only yummy but fun to eat, too. Simmered in a sweet soy-sauce mixture, they're easily one of the most popular foods in the islands.

Enchanted Forest Critters

- 1 tbsp soy sauce
- 1 tbsp sugar
- 1 or 2 slices SPAM
- 1 cup rice (pages 130 to 131)
- 1 piece nori
- 1 egg, beaten
- 1 tsp cornstarch
- 1 tsp sugar
- a few tsp extra-virgin olive oil

1. In a small pan, combine soy sauce and sugar with 1 tbsp water, stirring until the sugar dissolves. Simmer SPAM slices over medium-low heat 10 minutes or until they begin to turn a dark red brown color. Set aside to cool.

2. Meanwhile, use a mold or your hands to shape six petite rice balls into cubes. Cut the SPAM slices into squares and place one on top of each rice cube. Cut strips of nori and wrap them around the rice and spam, pasting down edges with water.

3. Run the egg through a sieve for a superfine texture. Dissolve the cornstarch in a few tsp of water and mix with egg and sugar. Warm oil in a pan over medium heat and cook egg until the bottom sets. Flip over, cook through, and set aside to cool. Use mini cutters to cut out various shapes and place one on top of each mini musubi. Cut out nori faces with a smiley-face punch.

Fried Noodles
Makes about 6 servings, enough for leftovers

- 1 tbsp olive oil
- ½ carrot, julienned
- 2 string beans, julienned
- 1 package noodles, such as yakisoba
- 2 tbsp oyster sauce
- pinch of salt

1. Heat oil in a pan on medium heat. Add carrots and beans and cook until tender.

2. Add noodles to the pan and stir fry a few minutes. Stir in oyster sauce and season with salt to taste. Cut noodles into smaller pieces with kitchen shears for easy eating.

3. Put a small portion into the bento box and garnish with a shooting star made out of parsley and leftover carrot.

Sugar snap peas and okra are attractive and healthy space fillers!

Flopsy, Mopsy, and Cottontail ⏱ 25 mins

Make this bento for a special some-bunny!

Bunny ears can be made out of anything from ham to cheese to fish sausage. Cut a zigzag edge into a green food divider to make your bunnies a grassy home in a vegetable garden decorated with carrot flowers.

Bunnies

- 3 rice balls (page 131)
- 1 slice thick-cut ham, cheese, or sausage
- 2 uncooked spaghetti noodles
- 1 sliver imitation crab (or ketchup)
- a few dabs of ketchup
- 1 piece nori
- 6 black sesame seeds

1. Place rice balls in the bento box. Use the legs of a gingerbread-man cutter to make six bunny ears out of ham. Break noodle into six small pieces. Stick them into the bottoms of the ears, and then push them into the rice balls.

2. Cut six red eyes out of imitation crab; use a dab of mayo to attach them to the rice. (Or just add dots of ketchup instead of crab.) Stick on six black eyes cut out of nori and six sesame-seed eyelashes.

3. Use a smiley face punch to make three nori smiles. Add a straight line and half a circle to each to make three bunny noses. Use a toothpick to dab on rosy ketchup cheeks.

Bacon-Wrapped Okra

- 1 piece bacon, cut in half lengthwise
- 1 okra pod, cooked and cut in half

1. Wrap each strip of bacon around a piece of okra and secure with toothpicks. Fry 3 minutes or until meat is crispy and sealed around the okra.

Vegetable Garden

- 1 cocktail wiener
- 2 or 3 bite-size cubes sweet potato
- 2 slices of carrot
- 3 broccoli florets
- about 15 green peas
- 1 okra pod
- 2 fish cakes or chicken nuggets, cooked
- 1 or 2 eggs, scrambled

1. Boil the cocktail wiener, sweet potato, sliced carrot, broccoli, peas, and okra; remove the wiener, okra, and peas after 1 minute, the broccoli after 2 minutes, and the sweet potato and carrots after 4 minutes. Reserve okra for bacon-wrapped okra.

2. Skewer the cocktail wiener and two fish cakes or chicken nuggets with decorative picks so they're easy to nibble. Arrange them in the bento box along with scrambled eggs, peas, broccoli, and sweet potato bites or other treats.

3. Use a mini cutter to shape carrots into flowers.

Cook the okra for bacon-wrapped okra along with the veggies!

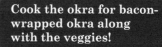

Goldilocks and the Three Bears

Six black sesame seeds make darling eyelashes for Mama Bear!

Scale down the portions if you're making this bento for a child's lunch, so it's not too big and not too small but just right! Fill the box with rice, strawberries, carrot sticks, a cherry tomato, and a small checkered apple (page 45). Three fiori pasta, cooked al dente, make a pretty flower garnish.

Goldilocks

- 1 piece nori
- ½ slice ham or bologna
- ½ slice cheddar cheese

1. Punch out nori faces for Goldilocks and all three bears using smiley face and bear punches. Set aside in a plastic zip-top bag.

2. Cut a circle out of ham. Cut hair out of cheese and arrange hair and curly bangs on top of the ham circle.

3. Cut a bow out of leftover ham. Apply Goldilocks' bow and facial features. Return to the same zip-top plastic bag and freeze until the bento box is ready.

Pork Cutlet (Tonkatsu)
Makes about 6 servings, enough for leftovers

- a few pinches of salt and pepper
- 6 boneless pork chops, thinly sliced
- flour for dusting
- 3 to 5 eggs, beaten
- 2 cups panko or regular bread crumbs
- several tbsp oil for frying

1. Salt and pepper the chops. Dust in flour, using a zip-top plastic bag for quick and easy coating and shaking off the excess. Dip chops in egg wash and then in the panko or bread crumbs. For thicker crust, dip in eggs and panko again.

2. In a frying pan, warm the oil over medium heat and fry the cutlets until golden brown, flipping once. Drain excess oil. Slice each cutlet into easy-to-eat squares. Stack a few in a corner of the bento box and put Goldilocks on top.

Three Bears

- ½ slice ham or bologna, left over from Goldilocks
- ½ slice white cheese

1. Use bear food cutters or a knife to cut two large bears and one mini bear out of ham. Cut two ovals out of cheese for Papa and Mama Bear's noses. Pinch a wide straw to cut a small oval for Baby Bear's nose.

2. Use the same straw to cut three more ovals, cut them in half, and add them to the bears' ears. Apply facial features. Arrange bears in the bento box.

To make curly hair and bangs, you can use the "arm with hand" cutter on a food cutter wheel.

I'm Bringin' Home a Baby Bumblebee

> For a teeny-tiny bumblebee, hard-boil a quail egg!

Add buzz to any boxed lunch: Just pack a cute little bumblebee egg with last night's leftovers—anything from pasta to mixed greens. This friendly bee is naturally tinted with broth and curry powder. He sits cheerily inside this bento box packed with tuna-fish salad (page 136), steamed broccoli, a few bite-size pieces of grilled fish, ham-wrapped asparagus (page 135), and mushrooms.

Bumblebee

- ¼ cup chicken or veggie broth
- 2 or 3 tsp curry powder (1 tsp for quail egg)
- 1 chicken or quail egg, hard-boiled and peeled
- 1 slice white cheese
- 1 piece ham
- 1 piece nori

1. Combine broth and curry powder in a bowl. Drop in the egg, cover, and refrigerate overnight or until egg is bright yellow.

2. When you're ready to pack the lunch, discard curry broth and cut a slit into the egg. Use a heart-shape cookie cutter to make bee's wings out of cheese. Freeze for a few minutes, and then tuck the point of the heart into the slit in the egg. Use a small straw to punch 2 small circles out of the ham to make rosy cheeks.

3. Cut bumblebee stripes out of nori. Press them on, along with eyes and a smile made with a smiley-face punch. Nestle the bee into the bento box once all other foods have been arranged.

❀ Freezing the cheese wings for a few minutes makes them easy to attach! See page 85 for how to do it.

Flower Garden

- 2 shitake mushrooms or 1 portobello mushroom
- 1 tsp butter
- ½ tsp soy sauce
- about 1 cup pink rice (page 130)
- 2 or 3 sugar snap peas or green beans, cut in half on the diagonal

1. Cut stars into the mushroom tops, making two cuts for each of the three lines in the star. Sauté the mushrooms in butter and soy sauce over medium-high heat until tender, about 3 minutes.

2. Scoop rice into the bento box. Arrange star-flower mushrooms and green beans on top to make a garden home for your bumblebee.

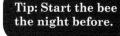

Tip: Start the bee the night before.

Ladybug Picnic

30 mins

Color your ladybugs yellow by mixing a crumbled hard-boiled egg yolk into white rice; or make them orange by adding a spoonful of ketchup.

What do you take to a Ladybug Picnic? How about savory chicken and veggies, a hard-boiled egg skewered with a food pick, a cheese and veggie filled rolled-up omelet (page 136), and two hot-dog tulips!

Ladybugs

- 2 pink rice balls (pages 130 to 131)
- 1 lettuce leaf
- 1 sheet nori

1. Put rice balls into the bento box on top of lettuce, making sure the ruffled edge shows.

2. Use scissors and a hole punch to make ladybug heads and spots out of nori. Cut one thin stripe to put down the middle of each ladybug's wings.

✿ Cut ladybug antennae out of dried konbu kelp or simply use four fried noodles (page 19).

Savory Chicken & Veggies

- 3 or 4 small broccoli florets
- 5 green beans or sugar snap peas
- 2 baby carrots, sliced
- a few tbsp extra-virgin olive oil
- 4 or 5 bite-size pieces chicken breast
- 1 or 2 mushrooms, such as shitake
- 1 tbsp soup stock
- ½ tsp soy sauce
- pinch of salt and pepper
- 1 tbsp cornstarch dissolved in 1 tbsp water

1. Boil broccoli, green beans, and carrot; remove beans after 1 minute, broccoli after 2 minutes, and carrots after 4 minutes. In oil over medium-high heat, sauté chicken and mushrooms with the cooked veggies, stock, soy sauce, salt, and pepper. Stir in cornstarch.

How to Make Hot-Dog Tulips

Sugar snap peas or green beans cut in half diagonally make pretty leaves for Hot-Dog Tulips!

❶ Using a knife, cut a mini hot dog or cocktail wiener in half.

❷ Cut a cross into the uncut ends.

❸ Boil for about 30 seconds, and the tulips will open up!

For a Hot-Dog Flower, make a cross in the cut side instead!

Little Elves

Thin slices of fried tofu, called *aburaage* ("fried tofu skins"), can be used as pouches for other foods, and they make adorable pointy hats for these fairy-tale friends. Lunch is complete with a rolled-up omelet (page 136), bacon-wrapped chicken dumplings, a few broccoli and cauliflower florets, and half a cherry tomato.

Little Elves

- 1 fried tofu skin, store-bought or home-made (pages 134 to 135), cut in half
- 2 rice balls (page 131)
- 1 piece nori
- 1 slice ham or bacon
- 1 lettuce leaf

1. Wrap each slice of fried tofu around each rice ball like a pointy hat. Cut nori with scissors to make hair, eyes, and smiles. Use a drinking straw to cut cheeks out of ham or bacon.

2. Arrange Little Elves in your bento box. Use pieces of the lettuce leaf to keep them separated from other foods.

❀ Black sesame seeds make cute teardrop-shape eyes! Or you can trace this pattern and cut them out of nori.

Bacon-Wrapped Chicken Dumplings

- ¼ cup onion, minced
- pinch of salt and pepper
- ½ tsp potato starch
- about 2 oz ground chicken
- 1 piece bacon, cut in half
- a few mushrooms, such as shimeji

1. Combine onion, salt and pepper, potato starch, and chicken. Use your hands to roll into two balls for dumplings. Wrap the dumplings with bacon and secure the ends with toothpicks.

2. Sauté the bacon-wrapped dumplings and mushrooms over low heat until golden brown. Put them into the bento box, tucking in extra veggies around the edges.

> Save time by sautéing a few mushrooms or other veggies in the pan with the bacon-wrapped chicken dumplings!

Little Red Hen

Curry powder, dashi, and red cabbage make natural food colorings!

"Who will help me eat this bento?" said the Little Red Hen. "I will!" said her barnyard friends—the lazy cat, the noisy duck, and the pudgy pig. Eggs shaped and colored to look like animals are a fun way to garnish anything from creamed tuna to egg salad or mixed greens.

Little Red Hen

- 1 slice roast beef or other deli meat
- 1 slice red bell pepper
- 1 slice orange bell pepper or carrot
- 1 piece nori
- ½ cup rice (page 130)
- 3 black sesame seeds

1. Cut a hen shape out of deli meat. Add a beak and comb cut out of bell pepper or carrot. Punch one small circle and cut a few little strips out of nori for her eye and feet.

2. Scoop rice into one corner of the bento box. Assemble the little red hen on top. Don't forget to drop a few sesame seeds in front of her!

Design your own lunches in a bento diary!

Barnyard Animals

- ½ cup chopped red cabbage
- 1 drop lemon juice
- 3 chicken or quail eggs, hard-boiled and peeled
- 1 tsp powdered dashi
- 1 tsp curry powder
- 1 piece nori
- 2 slices carrot
- 1 serving creamed tuna (pages 132 to 133) or another dish

1. Bring 1 cup water to a boil and add the cabbage, cooking 1 to 2 minutes. Remove cabbage with a slotted spoon and add lemon juice to the pink water. Soak an egg in the liquid until it turns pink.

2. Dilute the dashi and curry powder in 1 cup of water; soak an egg in it until it turns yellow.

❧ These eggs are tinted naturally, but you can use food coloring if pressed for time!

3. Cut all three eggs in half. Use half the pink egg to cut ears for the pig and the cat. Punch cat, duck, and pig faces out of nori. Cut carrot slices into duck feet and a beak.

4. Put a serving of creamed tuna along the bottom of the bento box, keeping it separated with a plastic food divider. Place the eggs on top (yolk-side down), and gently apply the nori and carrot features. Add fresh fruit to fill the box.

Little Red Riding Hood

 30 mins

Make peeled hard-boiled eggs—and teeny tiny quail eggs—into finger food by skewering them with cupcake picks or other decorative food picks.

You can pin on Red Riding Hood's flower with a piece of uncooked spaghetti: Stick it through the cheese flower and into the rice; snip it off at the surface. The moisture from the rice will make the noodle edible by lunchtime!

Once upon a time, there was a girl named Little Red Riding Hood who lived in a village near a forest. One morning, she put on her red cloak and ventured into the forest to visit her grandmother, carrying this tasty bento box in her basket!

Little Red Riding Hood & Her Basket

- 1 sheet nori
- 1 pink rice ball and 1 white rice ball (pages 130 to 131)
- 1 slice salami
- 1 slice white cheese
- 1 sprig of fresh chervil or parsley
- 1 small piece uncooked spaghetti noodle
- 2 lettuce leaves

1. Wrap thin strips of nori around the pink rice ball in a basket-weave pattern. Cut a half circle out of nori for her hair. Cut the salami into a rectangle; wrap it around half the white rice ball. Use a straw to cut two rosy cheeks out of leftover salami.

2. Cut two teardrop eyes and a smile out of nori. Use a mini flower cutter to make a cheese flower. Use a straw to cut the center out of left-over salami, and use the spaghetti to pin it to the hood on top of a sprig of parsley. Use a small straw to cut a cheese nose.

3. Put Little Red Riding Hood and her basket on top of the lettuce in the bento box.

Strawberry-Mint Flowers

- 2 or 3 strawberries
- a few sprigs fresh mint

1. Cut off strawberry stems and replace them with fresh mint for a rosy, edible bouquet.

Calamari Tempura

- a few pieces squid or shrimp
- 1 tbsp flour, plus more to dust
- a few sprigs fresh basil or parsley
- 1 baby carrot, thinly sliced
- a few tbsp extra-virgin olive oil

1. Chop squid or shrimp into thin strips. Dust with flour. Roughly chop the herbs.

2. To make a tempura batter, combine 1 tbsp flour with ½ tbsp ice water. Dip the squid or shrimp, carrots, and herbs in the batter. Fry them in oil over medium heat until crispy and golden brown.

Japanese Veggie Salad

- ½ cup daikon radish
- 3 baby carrots
- ¼ cup cucumber, peeled
- 1 tbsp mayo
- pinch of salt
- 1 tsp white sesame seeds

1. Cut thin sticks of daikon radish, carrot, and cucumber or other veggies. Stir in mayo, salt, and sesame seeds. Place salad in a cupcake cup to separate it from the other foods in the box.

When spring is in full bloom, there's magic in the air. Broccoli bouquets and pretty plum flowers are quick and easy to assemble. Pack them with last night's leftovers or grilled yellowtail with mushrooms and pickled sweet-and-sour tomatoes (page 135), garnished with a sprig of fresh basil.

Plum Flowers

- about 1½ cup rice (page 130)
- 3 Japanese pickled plums (*umeboshi*) or fresh cherry tomatoes

1. Use a flower mold to shape the rice into three flowers. Put one pickled plum or cherry tomato in the center of each flower. Arrange in the bento box with 2 or 3 broccoli bouquets.

> Keep flowers white by separating them from the grilled fish and tomatoes with a food divider.

Grilled Yellowtail with Mushrooms

- 1 small yellowtail fillet
- 2 mushrooms, such as shitake
- pinch of salt

1. Cut the fish into bite-size pieces. Sprinkle fish and mushrooms with salt.

2. In a pan over medium heat, grill fish and mushrooms until golden brown and cooked through, about 5 minutes; use a spatula to keep them from sticking to the pan. Let cool before adding to the bento box.

How to Make Flower Bouquets

Simple **green-and-yellow flowers** can be made with 5 kernels of corn and a pea!

Carrot flowers punched out of cooked carrot rounds with a flower cutter couldn't be easier!

Corn kernels, peas, and carrot flowers or stars make dazzling **broccoli bouquets**.

Mushroom Friends

It's easy to punch rosy cheeks out of salami using a drinking straw!

These happy toadstools are made of cheese and salami. Serve them over last night's leftovers or shrimp spaghetti with broccoli, crispy zucchini, and bell-pepper slices or other bite-size snacks.

Mushroom Friends

- 1 slice white cheese
- 1 slice salami
- 1 piece nori

1. Use a mushroom-shape mini cookie cutter to cut out two mushrooms each from the cheese and the salami.

2. Remove the stems from the salami mushrooms and randomly cut three holes into each with a straw. Reserve the cut holes. Place the salami caps onto the cheese mushrooms.

3. Punch out two faces from the nori and arrange on the cheese. Place two salami dots as cheeks.

Shrimp Spaghetti with Veggies

- 1½ oz spaghetti noodles
- 3 sugar snap peas or green beans
- 1 or 2 broccoli florets
- 3 or 4 shrimp, cleaned and deveined
- a few tbsp extra-virgin olive oil
- 1 tbsp ketchup
- salt and pepper
- a sprig of fresh parsley

1. Boil spaghetti with peas and broccoli. Remove the peas and broccoli after 1 minute and set aside. Drain the noodles and reserve the water; bring it to a boil again and add the shrimp, cooking about 30 seconds or until pink.

2. Warm oil in a pan. Add noodles and then shrimp and ketchup, stirring and seasoning with salt and pepper.

3. Place spaghetti into the bento box, pushing it to one side to leave room for broccoli and other side dishes. Cut pea pods in half and insert them in various spots in the spaghetti. Sprinkle with parsley and arrange mushroom friends on top.

❀ Add chopped garlic and tomato sauce for more tomato flavor!

Crispy Zucchini

- one-fourth of a zucchini
- pinch of salt
- 1 egg
- 1½ tsp parmesan cheese
- 1 spring of parsley, minced
- about ¼ cup flour
- 2 or 3 tbsp extra-virgin olive oil

1. Use a potato peeler to make stripes in the zucchini skin; cut the zucchini into thick slices, and sprinkle with salt.

2. Beat the egg with the minced parsley and grated cheese. Coat zucchini with flour and then dip it in egg wash.

3. Warm oil in a pan over medium heat. Fry the zucchini slices until golden. Set aside to cool before arranging in the bento box.

The Musubi Man

Fill open spaces with a fish-shape container of soy sauce, broccoli with carrot stars, and a food cup filled with seasonal mixed berries.

This little Musubi Man is upset because his fish is getting away! In Hawaii, a *musubi* is any nori-wrapped rice ball, and this little guy is the island's version of the gingerbread man. He gets into all kinds of adventures.

The Musubi Man Goes Fishing

- 1 sheet nori
- 1 triangular rice ball (page 131)
- a few drops of red food coloring
- 1 fish-shape egg (page 103)
- 2 lettuce leaves
- 1 cherry tomato

1. Cut a strip of nori with kitchen scissors. Wrap it around the bottom of the rice ball to make a shirt; a dab of water will secure the ends. Use craft punches to cut eyes, cheeks, and a round mouth out of the leftover nori.

2. Dilute drops of food coloring in a small cup of water. Soak the fish-shape egg until it turns pink, adding more coloring as needed. Pat dry with a paper towel.

3. Line the bento box with lettuce. Arrange the musubi man, fried fish, and the pink fish-shape egg or other foods. Use a skewered cherry tomato to separate the musubi man and his fish.

Fried Fish
Makes about 8 servings, enough for leftovers

- 1 lb white fish fillets
- a few pinches of salt and pepper
- ½ cup flour
- ¼ cup milk
- 1 egg
- ½ cup panko or fine bread crumbs
- a few tbsp oil for frying

1. Slice each fillet into 3 or 4 smaller fillets and wash. Pat dry and season with salt and pepper. Chill in the fridge 30 minutes.

2. Mix together the flour, milk, egg, and bread crumbs. Add more milk if the batter is too thick. Dip the fish in the batter and fry in oil over medium heat until browned on all sides.

Natural ways to dye eggs include soy sauce (brown), curry powder in broth (yellow), water left over from cooking beets or cabbage (pink), and pickled eggplant syrup (violet blue).

Peter Pan

🕐 | 30 mins

Save time by boiling broccoli, green beans, or other veggies along with the corn! Remove beans after 1 minute, broccoli and corn after 2 minutes. For added flavor, try sautéing the corn with 2 tsp extra-virgin olive oil and a pinch of salt.

You can make a green hat for Peter Pan out of a spinach leaf and a sprig of parsley. Three mini mushroom bites, two crunchy-fried potato dumplings, and a golden wedge of corn-on-the-cob complete this recipe for never-ending childhood adventures.

Peter Pan

- 1 rice ball (page 131)
- 1 crêpe-style omelet (page 134) or 1 slice cheddar cheese
- 1 uncooked spaghetti noodle
- 1 piece nori
- 1 small piece salami, prosciutto, or ham
- 1 spinach leaf
- 1 sprig of fresh parsley

1. Put rice ball into the bento box. Cut egg into rectangles. Pin them onto the rice ball with a piece of uncooked spaghetti (it will soften up by lunchtime).

2. Cut a smiley face out of nori. Use a straw to punch two cheeks out of meat. Use a spinach leaf as both a food divider and a little green cap for Peter Pan. Once everything has been arranged in the bento box, add a sprig of parsley to his cap.

Mini Mushroom Bites

- about ¼ cup small mushrooms, such as enoki (enokitake)
- 1 slice salami, prosciutto, or ham
- a few tsp extra-virgin olive oil

1. Roll mushrooms into a bundle inside the meat and secure the ends with toothpicks.

2. Heat oil in a pan. Sauté meat-wrapped mushrooms over medium heat until mushrooms turn golden and the meat is crispy. Let cool and cut into 3 or 4 pieces; tuck them into the bento box after the main dishes have been arranged.

❂ Delicately flavored and rich in antioxidants, enoki mushrooms have long, thin stems and tiny, button-size caps. They quickly absorb flavors of other foods.

Crunchy-Fried Potato Dumplings

- about 2 tsp minced onion
- about 1 oz ground pork
- 1 small potato, boiled and mashed
- ¼ tsp curry powder
- pinch of salt and pepper
- 1 tbsp panko or bread crumbs
- 2 tsp black sesame seeds
- 1 tbsp flour
- 1 egg, beaten
- oil for frying

1. Sauté onion and meat 1 or 2 minutes until thoroughly cooked. Mix mashed potato, onion and pork mixture, curry powder, salt, and pepper. Roll into dumplings with your hands.

2. In a small dish, combine bread crumbs and sesame seeds. Dip dumplings in flour, then in beaten egg, and then in sesame bread crumb mixture. Deep fry until golden brown. Pat dry with a paper towel before adding to the bento box.

Redheaded Princess

A crown-shape food pick transforms any bento character into food royalty!

This ginger-haired sweetheart will brighten anyone's day. Pack her into a bento box with this recipe for ginger chicken and veggies or your favorite stir-fry dish. Fill spaces with broccoli florets wrapped in lettuce to look like flower bouquets, hot-dog tulips, and a bright red cherry tomato skewered with a decorative pick.

Redheaded Princess

- 2 lettuce leaves
- 1 rice ball (page 131)
- 1 hot dog, cooked
- 1 sugar snap pea or green bean
- 2 broccoli florets
- 1 or 2 tsp extra-virgin olive oil
- 1½ oz spaghetti noodles, cooked
- 1½ tsp baby carrot, diced
- 1 tsp ketchup
- pinch of salt and pepper
- 1 piece nori

1. Line a bento box with lettuce and add the rice ball. Cut two thin slices of hot dog to make cheeks.

2. Boil the sugar snap pea and broccoli 1 minute; leave the broccoli in 2 minutes. Set broccoli aside. Cut the pea pod in half on the diagonal. Take out one pea to make the princess's nose; sauté the rest with the chicken.

3. Warm oil in a pan, and sauté the noodles with diced carrots, ketchup, salt, and pepper over medium heat.

4. Arrange the spaghetti on top of the rice to look like hair. Cut nori with scissors or a punch to make the eyes and smile. Place the pea in the center for the nose and add cheeks.

Ginger Chicken & Veggies

- 2 slices eggplant
- 4 or 5 bite-size pieces chicken breast
- 1 tbsp potato starch or flour
- 3 or 4 mushrooms, chopped
- 1 boiled pea pod, left over from Princess recipe
- ¼ tsp ginger, grated
- 1 clove garlic, finely chopped
- 1 or 2 tbsp soup stock
- pinch of salt and pepper

1. Using a vegetable peeler, cut stripes into the eggplant skin and then cut into bite-size pieces.

2. Dust chicken with potato starch or flour and sauté until golden brown, 1 to 2 minutes.

3. Add the eggplant, mushrooms, pea pod, grated ginger, garlic, soup stock, salt, and pepper to the chicken and sauté 2 to 3 more minutes. Scoop the chicken and vegetables into the bento box.

> Once you've sliced the hot dog to make rosy cheeks for the princess, use the leftover ends to make hot-dog tulips (page 65).

Secret Garden

Carrot butterflies flutter by three happy ham-and-cheese flowers.

A magical secret garden awaits you inside this bento box! You can make a sunny yellow sky, green grass, and brown garden dirt out of soboro or any type of scrambled eggs, green vegetables, and browned ground meat.

Smiling Flowers

- 1 thick slice ham or bologna
- ½ slice cheddar cheese
- 1 piece nori

1. Cut three large flowers from the ham and top them with three circles cut from the cheese.

2. Punch out three smiley faces from the nori. Apply them to the cheese. Refrigerate on a paper towel until the rest of the bento has been arranged.

Soboro-Style Chicken

- ¼ lb ground chicken
- 1½ tbsp soy sauce
- 1 tbsp sugar
- 1 tbsp mirin (or any cooking wine)
- 1 slice ginger

1. Simmer all ingredients in a saucepan over medium heat, stirring constantly with chopsticks or a fork until chicken is cooked and sauce is almost gone. Remove ginger and set aside mixture to cool.

> A soboro is any crumbly, seasoned meat, fish, or eggs. Try packing this chicken and egg soboro with rice-ball chickens (pages 20 to 21).

Sweet Soboro-Style Eggs with Veggies

- 1 tsp sugar
- ¼ tsp salt
- ½ tsp mirin (or any cooking wine)
- 2 eggs, beaten
- 1 tsp extra-virgin olive oil
- about 1 cup rice (page 130)
- 3 broccoli florets, cooked
- 3-inch section of cucumber
- 3 carrot slices

1. Add sugar, salt, and mirin to the eggs. Warm oil in a pan over medium heat and add egg mixture. Stir constantly with chopsticks to create small crumbles of scrambled egg. Set aside to cool.

2. Add rice to bento box in a flat layer. Add soboro-style chicken to the bottom section. Cover the rest of the rice with the sweet scrambled eggs.

3. Break the broccoli florets apart and tuck in between the scrambled eggs and meat so the broccoli tops look like grass.

4. Slice off cucumber skin and cut 3 thin strips to make flower stems. Cut out leaves with a knife or leaf-shape food cutter. Use a mini butterfly cutter to make the carrot slices into butterflies. Place them around the flowers.

With a little kitchen magic, you can fit an entire winter wonderland into a bento box!

This happy little polar bear lives on an itty bitty glacier made of salmon-flavored rice. Sautéed pork and mushrooms taste great with shredded cabbage, a few steamed broccoli florets, and a skewered cherry tomato.

Teeny Tiny Polar Bear

- 1 cup seasoned rice (page 130)
- 1 slice cheese
- 1 quail egg, hard-boiled and peeled
- a few dabs of ketchup
- 1 piece nori

1. Scoop rice into the bento box. Make ears out of cheese and tuck them into the egg. Use a straw to make a cheese nose, and stick it on with a dab of ketchup.

2. Stick nori eyes and smile onto the egg and use a toothpick to dab on rosy ketchup cheeks.

Sautéed Pork & Mushrooms

- 1 tsp soy sauce
- 1 tsp sake
- ¼ tsp mirin (or cooking wine)
- ¼ tsp ground ginger
- 1 or 2 tsp extra-virgin olive oil
- 1 oz pork, cut into bite-size pieces
- ½ oz mushrooms, stems trimmed

1. Combine soy sauce, sake, mirin, and ground ginger; set aside.

2. Heat oil in a pan over medium-high heat. Sauté pork and mushrooms until tender. Add the soy sauce mixture and simmer until the pork is browned. Let cool before scooping into the bento box. Arrange veggies and nestle the polar bear on top.

How to Tuck Cheese into an Egg

❶ Cut little ears out of cheese with a toothpick. Freeze them a few minutes to make them stiff and easy to work with.

❷ Use a knife to make a slit in the top third of the egg.

❸ With tweezers, tuck the cheese into the slit in the egg.

❹ Done!

Three Little Pigs

Three little pigs go "Wee, wee, wee," all the way home! Make them snug in their bento box by filling in spaces with half a round of corn-on-the-cob (page 47), a few steamed broccoli florets, and a wedge of bright red cherry tomato.

Three Piggies

- 1 or 2 lettuce leaves
- 3 pink rice balls (pages 130 to 131)
- 1 slice cheddar cheese
- 1 piece nori

1. Line a bento box with lettuce. Arrange rice balls.

2. Use a wide straw to cut three snouts from the cheese; use a thin straw to make nostrils (page 39). Make three more ovals with the wide straw, and then cut them in half to make ears.

3. Use a smiley-face punch or kitchen scissors to cut eyes and smiles out of nori and arrange piggie faces.

❁ Flatten the straw to make an oval shape.

Chicken and Veggie Roll

- 2 or 3 oz chicken breast, sliced in half lengthwise
- pinch of salt and pepper
- 2 sprigs fresh sage or other herbs
- 1 tbsp flour
- 1 egg, beaten
- about ¼ cup bread crumbs
- a few tbsp extra-virgin olive oil

1. Flatten the chicken with a rolling pin and sprinkle with salt and pepper. Scatter herbs over the chicken and roll it, securing the end with toothpicks. Dust with flour, coating all sides.

2. Dip the roll into the egg and then roll it in bread crumbs. Warm the oil in a pan. Over medium-high heat, fry the roll 4 to 5 minutes or until cooked through.

3. Pull out the toothpicks and slice the roll in half. Tuck it into the bento box.

Roll up your favorite cheese or in-season herbs into a chicken roll or croquette!

Twinkle, Twinkle Little Star

 20 mins

Thank your lucky stars for this quick and easy way to make leftovers sparkle!

Easy-to-make lucky stars brighten up last night's leftovers like this pizza, or a slice of low-fat turkey lasagna. Broccoli, cherry tomatoes, and green peas cut in half on the diagonal are a pretty way to fill empty spaces in the bento box. You can use a food divider or lettuce leaf to separate the kiwi and orange slices.

Lucky Stars

- 1 slice cheese
- 1 piece nori
- 1 serving leftover pizza or low-fat turkey lasagna

1. Use cookie cutters or trace the shape below to make stars out of cheese. Punch three smiley faces out of nori and attach them to the stars. Set aside (or freeze) on a paper towel until you're ready to pack the bento box.

2. Cut leftover pizza into easy-to-nibble slices. Arrange stars on top.

Low-Fat Turkey Lasagna
Makes about 6 servings, enough for leftovers

- 1 (1-lb) box lasagna noodles
- 1 lb ground turkey
- 1 (26-oz) jar spaghetti or marinara sauce
- 2 cups cottage cheese
- 2 cups mozzarella cheese

1. Preheat oven to 350°F. Boil lasagna noodles al dente.

2. In a pan over medium-high heat, sauté ground turkey until brown. Stir in spaghetti sauce and simmer for 15 minutes.

3. Layer lasagna noodles, meat sauce, and cheeses in a 9-by-13-inch pan. Cover with foil and bake 1 hour, removing the foil for the last 10 minutes. Let lasagna cool before cutting into squares and packing into your bento box, with lucky stars on top.

✿ Don't let hot food melt your cheese stars! Make sure it's fully cooled before you start packing.

Japanese nori punches or smiley-face craft punches (used for scrapbooking) are a quick way to cut happy faces out of nori.

Special Day Treats

We love Cuties & Critters and Fairy-Tale Friends, but some days require something extra extraordinary. These themed bento boxes are a yummy and nutritious way of celebrating holidays, birthdays, events, and big trips: You can pack healthy snacks for Halloween and Easter, personalize a birthday bento box, or simply brighten up someone's rainy day with a special lunch-time treat.

Autumn Leaves

15 mins

Don't forget to pack a little sauce container filled with salad dressing!

When the air gets nippy and leaves turn red, brown, and gold, it's time to make a special seasonal bento box! Choose fall-colored foods, such as red and yellow tomatoes, carrots, spaghetti and meat sauce, and cheddar cheese.

Happy Autumn Leaves

- 1 slice cheddar cheese
- 1 piece nori
- 1 cup noodles, cooked al dente
- ½ cup meat sauce, cooked and cooled

1. Cut leaves from the cheese. Apply faces punched out of nori. Set aside (or freeze) on a paper towel until ready to use.

2. Place noodles in your bento box; if you're using spaghetti, curl the noodles with a fork to neatly tuck in the ends.

3. Spoon cooled sauce over the noodles (hot sauce would melt cheese leaves!). Arrange the leaves on top.

❀ Leaf-shape noodles—plus snowflake-shape noodles, flower-shape noodles, and more—are available in many supermarkets and online. Use them as a main dish or pretty garnish.

Mini Salad & Fruits

- 2 lettuce leaves
- 1 baby carrot, sliced
- 1 yellow grape tomato, halved
- 1 or 2 strawberries
- about ¼ cup blueberries
- 3 raspberries or cherries

1. Tear the lettuce leaves into small pieces and arrange in the bento box. Layer carrot slices on top. Tuck yellow grape tomato halves into the lettuce.

2. Put strawberries into the box, top down. Drop blueberries into remaining space and top with three raspberries, adding more blueberries to fill space.

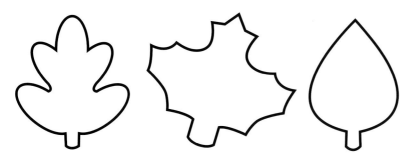

Use tracing paper or mini cookie cutters to make tons of fun shapes from cheese!

Beach Party Hot Dog

These little cheese guys are happy to swim on a surfboard made out of a hot dog bun, hamburger, or any type of sandwich—as long as you put them into a bento box and take them with you to the beach!

Beach Party Hot Dog

- 1 bun
- mayo, ketchup, or other condiments
- hot dog
- 1 lettuce leaf
- 1 slice cheddar cheese
- 1 piece nori

1. Slice open the bun. Spread condiments inside. Add the hot dog and lettuce, making sure the ruffled lettuce edge sticks out like a wave.

2. Use a gingerbread-man cookie cutter to punch two little guys out of cheese. Use a smiley-face punch or scissors to make faces out of nori. Extra eyes make cute buttons. Dab on cute ketchup cheeks with a toothpick.

3. Press these happy swimmers onto the condiments inside the bun.

If the smiley faces don't stick, dab a little mayo or ketchup between them and the cheese.

You can use tracing paper or a gingerbread-man cookie cutter to make two little cheese swimmers.

Sliced fruit can be cut with cookie cutters into butterflies or other shapes. Sprinkle with lemon juice to preserve color.

Pack these teddy bear buddies into a bento box with slices of teriyaki beef, tasty crab and pea eggs, or scrambled eggs. Fill the second tier of the box (or an extra storage container) with fresh snacks, such as steamed broccoli, a checkered apple (page 45), peeled and quartered kiwi, cherries, and sweet-potato butterflies.

Teddy Bears

- 1 tsp soy sauce
- ¾ cup rice (page 130)
- ¼ cup bonito flakes (optional)
- 3 lettuce leaves
- 1 slice white cheese
- 1 piece nori

1. Mix soy sauce with rice until evenly colored. Shape rice into two bear shapes with your hands or a mold.

2. Roll bears in bonito flakes if you like. Line the bento box with lettuce leaves and arrange bears on top.

3. Cut two large ovals out of cheese for their muzzles. Use a pinched straw to punch two small ovals out of the cheese scraps; cut in half to make ears. Add to bears, and then add eyes, noses, and mouths.

❀ Use a hole punch to cut six circles out of nori for eyes and noses. Use four nori-punch smiles to make the mouths. Keep all your tiny nori pieces safe in a snack-size zip-top plastic bag!

⌣ + ○ + ⌣ = ୧

Teriyaki Beef

- 2 tbsp soy sauce
- 1 tbsp sugar
- 1 tbsp mirin (or any cooking wine)
- pinch minced garlic
- pinch grated ginger
- 1 thin slice of beef
- 1 pat butter

1. Combine soy sauce, sugar, mirin, garlic, and ginger in a bowl. Add the beef and marinate 30 minutes.

2. Warm butter in a pan over medium-high heat. Panfry the beef until slightly browned on both sides. Once the meat has cooled, chop it into strips with kitchen scissors and arrange it in the bento box.

Crab & Pea Eggs

- 1 egg
- 1 tbsp milk
- 1 stick imitation crab, finely chopped
- a few tsp extra-virgin olive oil
- a small handful of peas

1. Beat egg and milk. Add crab to egg mixture. Heat oil in a pan. Fry the egg mixture, stirring constantly with chopsticks to break egg into small crumbles. Add peas and continue cooking until eggs are done.

Happy Birthday! Make this bento box as an edible gift on someone's special day. Use a food divider to separate the rice present from other snacks, such as bacon-wrapped green beans (page 134), cooked spinach, cherry tomatoes, and a rolled-up omelet that uses the leftover scraps of veggies, meat, and cheese.

Present & Bunny Ribbon

- 1 slice white cheese
- 1 piece ham or salami
- 1 piece nori
- a dab of ketchup
- 1 to 2 tsp black sesame seeds
- pinch of salt
- 1 cup rice (page 130)
- about 1 tsp black sesame seeds

1. Use a cookie cutter to punch a crinkle-cut circle out of cheese. Use a mini bunny cutter to cut a pink bunny out of ham. Place the bunny on the cheese. Use a drinking straw to cut a small nose from the leftover cheese and place on the bunny. Punch three dots from the nori and place on the bunny as eyes and a nose.

2. Use a toothpick to dab on a little ketchup for cheeks. Create a dotted border by pressing sesame seeds or little rectangles cut from nori into the cheese.

3. Mix sesame seeds and a pinch of salt into the rice. Scoop rice into the bento box and flatten the surface. Cut ribbons out of nori with kitchen scissors and arrange over the rice; top it off with a sprinkle of sesame seeds and the bunny ribbon.

❀ Make a red, white, and green Christmas ribbon with cheese, lettuce, and red pepper!

Cooked Spinach

- a big handful of spinach leaves
- pinch of salt
- dash of soy sauce
- 1 tsp bonito flakes or red pepper flakes
- 1 tsp sesame seeds

1. Boil water with a pinch of salt and add spinach, cooking 30 seconds. Drain well and roughly chop.

2. Sprinkle the spinach with soy sauce to taste and add a pinch of bonito flakes or red pepper flakes and sesame seeds. Place in a food cup and add to the box.

Mince the leftover cheese, ham, and green beans. Beat with an egg and make a rolled-up omelet (page 134).

Boy's Day

🕐 | 15 mins

The fish flag can be made with layered ham and cheese instead of fish cake: Color cheese with food pens or food coloring if you like.

Boy's Day, or *Tango no Sekku*, is celebrated on May 5 in Japan and Hawaii. It's now known as Children's Day, or *Kodomo no hi*, but the displaying of cloth fish is still a great way to celebrate male children.

Happy Boy

- ½ cup blue rice (page 130)
- 2 or 3 lettuce leaves
- ½ slice bologna
- 1 piece nori

1. Scoop blue rice into the bento box; flatten the surface to accommodate the boy and his fish. Line the remaining space with lettuce leaves.

2. Cut out a head with ears from bologna. Use scissors to cut the boy's hair out of nori. Use a smiley-face punch to make a face. Apply face and hair.

Three-Fish Flag

- 3 pieces fish cake, thinly sliced
- red, blue, and green food coloring
- 1 uncooked spaghetti noodle

1. Use a knife to cut three wavy rectangles out of fish cake. Cut notches into the ends to make tails.

2. Cut a piece of drinking straw lengthwise to make a C-shape cutter. Press it into the fish to create fish scales. Soak fish cakes in a 1-to-1 solution of food coloring and water.

3. Use a straw to cut out eyes from the fish cake scraps and apply one to each fish. Punch three dots out of nori with a hole punch and apply to fish eyes. Arrange noodle and the three fish to make a colorful flag.

Teriyaki Meatballs

Makes about 8 servings, enough to share with buddies!

- 2 slices bread
- 2 tbsp milk
- 2 lb ground beef
- 1 lb ground chicken
- 1 carrot, finely grated
- 1 onion, minced
- 1 tsp salt
- 1 tsp pepper
- 1 egg
- oil for frying

Teriyaki Sauce

- ½ cup soy sauce
- 5 tbsp sugar

1. Moisten the bread with milk in a large bowl. Combine with the remaining ingredients and shape into balls. Heat oil in a pan over medium heat and panfry the meatballs until cooked through.

2. While meatballs are cooking, make the teriyaki sauce: Mix the soy sauce and sugar in a bowl. When meatballs are done, add to the bowl of sauce and soak 5 to 10 minutes. Pierce soaking meatballs with a fork to let the sauce into the middle. Drain meatballs before adding to the bento box.

❀ Cup meatballs in a lettuce leaf. Add berries, broccoli with carrot stars, and a food pick stacked with edamame.

10 mins

Cut the ends off baby carrots and quarter them lengthwise for baby carrot sticks!

Beep beep! Bento boxes are a great way to eat yummy, homemade foods on long road trips. And custom bento boxes and egg molds—shaped like cars, animals, or popular cartoon characters—make everyday leftovers lots of fun. This cool car bento is lined with lettuce and then packed with a car-shape egg, Hamburger Helper topped with cheesy letters, baby carrot sticks, and mixed berries.

Car Trip

- 1 car-shape egg
- a few drops blue food coloring
- 3 lettuce leaves
- 1 cup leftover Hamburger Helper, pasta, or chili
- 1 slice cheddar cheese
- 3 baby carrots, quartered
- 1 cherry tomato
- mixed berries

1. Soak the car-shape egg in water with food coloring for 10 minutes. Let the coloring soak in, and then pat dry with a paper towel.

2. Line the left side of the bento box with lettuce leaves. Drop in Hamburger Helper until almost full. Top with cheese letters spelling VROOM or BEEP BEEP!

3. Cup the car-shape egg with lettuce and tuck into the box. Arrange baby carrot sticks, cherry tomato, and mixed berries. A condiment bottle can hold soy sauce or salad dressing.

How to Use an Egg Mold to Make Fun Shapes

Egg molds come in all sorts of shapes: cars, fish, and more!

❶ Hard-boil an egg, peeling it before it cools completely.

❷ While the hard-boiled egg is still warm, put it into the mold.

❸ Snap the lid shut and soak the mold in ice water 10 to 15 minutes.

❹ Open the lid. Trim off edges if necessary. Done!

35 mins

Happy Christmas! These little penguins are waiting for Santa Claus. You can fill this holiday-themed bento box with bacon-wrapped cauliflower, a few pieces of simmered squash (page 136), broccoli, and a fresh cherry tomato!

Christmas Penguins

- 1 sheet nori
- 1 slice carrot, cooked
- 1 uncooked spaghetti noodle
- 1 slice imitation crab (*kanikama*) or ham
- 2 rice balls (page 131)

❀ Imitation crab makes a cute santa cap—and the salty flavor of yummy crab tastes great with rice. But you can make a Santa hat out of ham, salami, or the tip of a red bell pepper.

1. Trace the penguin shape. Fold a nori sheet in half and, using kitchen scissors, cut out two penguin shapes at once. Press them onto the rice balls. Use a hole punch to make four eyes out of the leftover nori.

2. Cut the carrot slice in half; trim the halves to look like beaks. Pin carrot beaks onto the rice balls with 2 small pieces of uncooked spaghetti (moisture from the rice will soften it up by lunchtime). Use scissors to neatly snip off the ends of the noodles. Put penguins into the bento box.

3. Use a wide straw to punch four rosy cheeks out of crab or ham.

4. Fillet the crab and wrap it around one of the penguin's heads to make a Santa hat.

Bacon-Wrapped Cauliflower

- 2 or 3 cauliflower florets
- 1 slice bacon
- 1 tsp extra-virgin olive oil

1. Boil cauliflower 3 minutes, drain water. Roll bacon around each cauliflower floret and secure the ends with a toothpick.

2. Warm oil in a pan over medium heat. Sauté bacon-wrapped cauliflower 2 minutes or until the bacon is crispy and golden brown. Arrange around Christmas Penguins in the bento box.

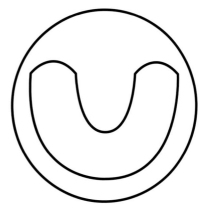

Early-Bird Omelet

Pack a pretty early-bird omelet, chicken-and-veggie rolls, and a yummy cheesy sausage (page 134) for breakfast anytime! Leftover cheese and veggies can be folded inside the omelet or placed into gaps in the bento box.

Early-Bird Omelet

- 1 or 2 eggs, beaten
- a few tsp extra-virgin olive oil
- ½ cup cheese, veggies, cooked rice, or other fillings
- 2 slices cheese, 1 white, 1 cheddar
- a few sprigs parsley, chervil, or basil
- 1 piece nori
- a few black sesame seeds
- 1 sliced carrot, cooked

1. Run the egg through a strainer so the color and texture are smooth. Warm oil in a pan over low heat until the egg is almost cooked, about 30 seconds. Add fillings to one half, fold the omelet, and cook a few more seconds. Put it into the bento box.

2. Use a mini flower cutter to cut the white cheese and a small straw to punch flower centers out of cheddar cheese. Arrange herb leaves on the omelet and place flowers on top. Garnish with sesame seeds.

3. Cut a bird shape out of nori with scissors. Put it on top of cheese [a] and cut around the edges with a toothpick [b]. Add a thin half-moon carrot at the bird's throat.

Chicken & Veggie Rolls

- 2 or 3 oz chicken breast, cooked
- 5 or 6 cooked carrots, broccoli, or green beans
- pinch of salt and pepper
- about 1 tbsp flour

1. Flatten chicken with a rolling pin, put a few veggies on top, and sprinkle with salt and pepper.

2. Roll up and fasten with a toothpick. Dust with flour and sauté until crispy. Cut into 2 or 3 rounds and arrange in the bento box. Use mini cutters to punch butterflies out of the remaining carrots. Arrange extra veggies, such as asparagus, broccoli, tomato, and butterfly-shape carrots, in the spaces around the omelet and rolls.

If you need to finish packing the rest of your bento box, freeze the little sparrow in a zip-top plastic baggie until you're ready. Chilling it keeps the pieces in place, and they'll be room temperature by lunchtime.

a

b

Easter Baskets

This recipe makes 10 mini sandwiches, so you'll have enough to share with family, friends, or schoolmates. Use themed cookie cutters for different holidays.

Candy-centric holidays such as Easter usually mean an overabundance of sugar. Give your family something different by packing little snack bentos: egg-shape egg salad sandwiches decorated with cheese chicks and bunnies, plus mini carrot and celery sticks, packaged cheese cubes, and Jell-O eggs!

Egg Salad Sandwiches

- 10 bread slices
- 5 eggs, hard-boiled and peeled
- a few tbsp mayo
- pinch of salt and pepper
- about 5 yellow and white cheese slices
- 5 lettuce leaves

1. Cut two egg shapes from each slice of bread and set aside. Dice eggs and mix in mayo, salt, and pepper to taste. Sandwich the egg-salad mixture with the egg-shape bread.

2. Cut bunnies and chicks out of cheese and decorate with nori smiley faces or a food marker.

3. Line each bento box with lettuce leaves and place one sandwich in each. Top sandwiches with bunnies and chicks and then add mini carrot and celery sticks, Tiny Jell-O eggs, and other healthy treats.

Tiny Jell-O Eggs

- 2 (3.3-oz) packages Jell-O

1. Lightly grease a Jell-O bean mold with cooking spray or vegetable oil applied with a paper towel. Put mold on an even, flat surface.

2. Empty Jell-O into a glass measuring cup that has a spout (for easy pouring) and then stir in 1¼ cups boiling water. Continue stirring until the powder dissolves. Carefully pour the mixture into each bean mold.

3. Refrigerate 30 minutes or until firm. To remove the beans, lightly moisten your fingers and press them out.

❀ Repeat with several colors to make a rainbow of tiny Jell-O eggs!

Try making a hatching chick out of an egg.
See page 138 for directions.

Girl's Day

🕐 | 15 mins

Learn how to make Apple Bunnies on page 49!

Observed in Japan and Hawaii on March 3, Girl's Day (*Hinamatsuri*) celebrates a young girl's growth and happiness. Make her smile with this happy little rice-ball girl! Plus a serving of mochiko chicken, fresh sliced fruits, Potato Flowers, and an adorable Apple Bunny.

Happy Girl

- 2 lettuce leaves
- 1 orange rice ball (pages 130 to 131)
- 1 piece nori

1. Line the bento box with lettuce leaves. Place the rice ball in one corner.

2. Use a smiley-face punch or scissors to make a face out of nori. Cut thin strips of leftover nori to use as hair.

Potato Flowers

- 1 small baked potato or sweet potato
- pinch of salt

1. Peel and slice the potato. Cut into flower shapes. Place the potato scraps into a corner of the bento box, breaking them apart as needed. Layer potato flowers on top; sprinkle with salt.

❀ Trace this flower pattern or use a food cutter to make potato flowers. If available in your area, try using Okinawan sweet potato for a burst of purple color!

Mochiko Chicken
Makes about 8 servings, enough for leftovers

- 2 lb boneless, skinless chicken thighs, cut into pieces
- 4 tbsp mochiko flour (sweet rice flour)
- 4 tbsp cornstarch
- 4 tbsp sugar
- 5 tbsp soy sauce
- 2 eggs
- ¼ cup chopped green onions
- ½ tsp salt
- 2 cloves garlic, grated

1. Combine all ingredients in a heavy-duty zip-top plastic bag and marinate in the refrigerator overnight.

2. In a large, heavy pot, add about an inch of oil and heat. Fry chicken in oil until light brown, turning pieces often to prevent sugar from burning.

❀ Mochiko flour, also known as sweet rice flour, can be found at major supermarkets and Asian groceries. It is gaining in popularity worldwide because it adds gluten-free sweetness to any dish!

I  You

🕐 | **20 mins**

If you don't have a sushi mat, use a piece of aluminum foil!

A bento lunch is often viewed as a symbol of love. Pack even more affection into a heart-themed bento for a special someone! Fill it to the brim with sliced nectarines, strawberries, and other treats.

Sweetheart Sushi
Makes 2 servings (6 rolls), enough to share

- 1 tbsp sushi vinegar (page 132)
- 1 cup pink rice, hot (page 130)
- ½ sheet nori
- 2 lettuce leaves
- 1 slice deli meat

1. Mix sushi vinegar into the rice.

2. Lay the nori on a sushi mat. Spread the rice over it [a]. Spoon shrimp mixture down the middle; then roll the ends into the middle, forming a long roll [b]. Slice off the ends and cut three 1-inch slices. Cut each slice in half [c] and shape into a heart [d].

3. Line the bento box with lettuce leaves. Add three heart-shape sushi. Cut three hearts out of deli meat. Punch out three nori faces and stick them onto the meat, and place on top of sushi.

Miso Chicken

- 1 tbsp miso
- 1 tbsp mirin (or any cooking wine)
- 1 tsp soy sauce
- about 1 tsp extra-virgin olive oil
- 1 chicken thigh, cut into bite-size pieces

1. Combine miso, mirin, and soy sauce in a zip-top plastic bag. Marinate chicken at least 30 minutes.

2. Warm oil in a pan and brown the chicken over medium-high heat until cooked through. Let cool before adding to the bento box.

Use a heart cutter or trace this shape for the deli meat.

Pancake Mouse

Use a pick to secure the egg to the breakfast sandwich and make a cute mouse tail!

A tiny mouse says good morning to you! To transform everyday pancakes into a cute and yummy pancake sandwich, use a sugar-free pancake mix and layers of crispy bacon, scrambled eggs, cheese, and fresh lettuce.

Mouse

- 1 small piece of ham or cheese
- 1 chicken or quail egg, hard-boiled and peeled
- 1 piece nori

1. Assemble a pancake sandwich or another snack for your mouse to perch on.

2. Using a fat straw or bottle cap, punch two circles out of ham. Put them into a plastic zip-top bag and freeze for a few minutes; they'll be stiff and much easier to insert into the egg.

3. Slice off a small sliver of the egg from top to bottom, so it will lay flat on the pancake. Make a slit almost halfway through the egg. Using tweezers, gently insert the circles into the slit in the egg, making two mouse ears. (See how on page 85.)

4. Use scissors or a paper punch to cut 2 eyes and a wee little mouse nose out of nori. Gently apply facial features to the egg.

Tint an egg pink and insert long ears to make a pretty pink brunch bunny! See how on pages 77 and 85.

Pancake Sandwich

- 2 pats of butter
- about 1 cup pancake batter, made from a sugar-free mix
- 2 tsp ketchup or other condiments
- 2 eggs, beaten
- 1 slice cheddar cheese
- 1 or 2 slices bacon
- 2 lettuce leaves

1. Warm 1 pat of butter in a pan over medium-high heat. Pour batter into 3 small circles. Once the bottoms are firm and golden brown, flip pancakes with a spatula. Grill the other side. Move pancakes onto a paper towel to cool.

2. Warm another pat of butter in a pan over medium-low heat. Add eggs and scramble until cooked through; stir in cheese or other extras if desired. Grill bacon about 2 minutes per side, or until slightly brown and crispy.

3. Assemble the sandwich: Spread the top of a pancake with ketchup or other condiments, layer with scrambled eggs and lettuce. Add the next pancake, topped with more lettuce, a slice of cheddar cheese, and bacon folded in half (to fit). Top with the third pancake.

Pizza Party!

 15 mins

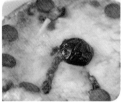

Try a **shooting star pizza** with a ham star and a basil leaf; a **clock pizza** with 12 pepperoni and two asparagus stalks; a **flower** made of **sausage** and a black olive; or **smiley faces** with a slice of boiled potato or cheese on top of a fresh basil leaf!

It's time for a pizza party! Pack mini pizzas into a bento box or make them at lunchtime with children. Everyone can choose favorite toppings.

Tiny Flowers Pizza

- 1 individual-size pizza crust or English muffin
- a few tbsp pizza sauce
- ⅓ cup grated mozzarella cheese
- mushrooms, red onions, parsley, black olives, or other toppings
- 1 or 2 flower-shape eggs
- 1 thick slice of cheese
- 4 red pepper flakes

1. Top the pizza with sauce, grated cheese, and mushrooms or toppings of your choice. Cut the flower-shape eggs in half and arrange on top of the pizza, yolk-side up. Toast the pizza in the oven at 350°F for 5 minutes or until crust is toasted and cheese is melted.

2. Use a mini flower cutter to make four flowers out of the thick slice of cheese. Add them to the hot pizza and put a red pepper flake in the center of each.

How to Make Flower-Shape Eggs

❶ You need a peeled hard-boiled quail egg, a mini flower mold, and a plastic fork or spoon with a blunt end.

❷ While the egg is still hot, place it in the mold.

❸ Use the blunt end of the fork to gently push the egg through the mold.

❹ Done! Chill eggs for a few minutes to set the shape.

Rainy day, go away! This yummy bento packed with summer squash (page 136), broccoli, cauliflower, tomato, and chicken dumplings will help bring back sunny skies.

Umbrellas and Raindrops

- 2 rice balls (page 131)
- 1 slice bologna or fish sausage
- 1 piece nori
- 1 slice deli meat

1. Line the bento box with lettuce leaves. Place rice balls on top.

2. Cut two circles out of bologna. Use kitchen scissors to cut a wide drinking straw into a half circle [a]. Use the straw to cut curves into each umbrella's bottom edge [b]. Cut two umbrella handles out of the leftover meat [c].

3. Use a hole punch to make polka dots out of nori. Place them on top of each umbrella [d]. Use a kitchen knife or mini cookie cutter to make raindrops out of deli meat.

Chicken Dumplings

- about 2½ oz ground chicken
- 1 tsp minced onion
- 1 to 2 fresh minced chives
- 1 tsp potato starch
- pinch of salt
- a few tsp oil

1. Combine ground chicken, onion, chives, starch, and salt. Roll the mixture into 2 dumplings.

2. Warm oil in a pan over medium-high heat. Sauté dumplings until golden brown, allow to cool, and tuck them into the bento box.

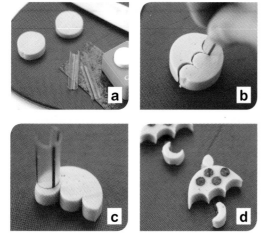

> You can make umbrellas and raindrops out of any deli meat, sausage, or cheese!

Sailboat

Sail away for the day and take a bento box packed with a balanced lunch: bite-size beef croquettes, broccoli, and carrot fishes. Once the main dishes are packed, tuck in orange slices, broccoli, and a cherry tomato skewered with a food pick.

Sailboat

- 1 slice bologna
- 1 or 2 slices white cheese
- 1 cup blue rice (page 130)
- a few lettuce leaves

1. Use a circle cookie cutter to cut a circle from the bologna; cut it in half to make the bottom of the boat. Use a knife or toothpick to cut two triangles out of the cheese. Color or decorate the cheese sails as desired or leave them white.

2. Add the blue rice to the bento box, pushing it to one side and flattening the surface. Separate it from the other half of the box with a lettuce leaf, and arrange the beef croquettes and broccoli before topping the rice with the sailboat.

Beef Croquettes
Makes about 8, enough for leftovers

- 2 tsp garlic salt
- 2 tbsp sugar
- 2 tsp oyster sauce
- 1 tbsp ketchup
- 1 tbsp Worcestershire sauce
- 1 tbsp mirin (or cooking wine)
- a few tbsp extra-virgin olive oil
- 1 onion, minced
- 1 lb hamburger
- 3 large potatoes, boiled
- ¼ cup flour
- 3 to 5 eggs, beaten
- 2 cups panko or bread crumbs
- oil for frying

1. Combine the garlic salt, sugar, oyster sauce, ketchup, Worcestershire sauce, and mirin and mix well. Set aside.

2. Heat olive oil in a pan and sauté onion until tender. Add the hamburger and cook until browned. Add the seasoning mixture and simmer 5 minutes. While this is cooking, mash the potatoes, pressing through a strainer to get a fine texture.

3. Simmer another 5 minutes. Mix the beef mixture into the mashed potatoes. Cover and refrigerate until cooled.

4. Roll the mixture into balls, dredge in flour, dip in egg wash, and coat in panko. Deep fry the croquette balls until golden brown.

For low-fat croquettes, replace the beef with ground turkey!

Sprinkle cut fruit with lemon juice to preserve color!

When school is out for a snow day, it's time to make a snowman out of rice balls, ham, and a tiny carrot nose. Fill the bento box with yummy fried shrimp, sliced sweet potato, cherry tomatoes, broccoli, and sliced sugar snap peas. Add sliced peaches and half a strawberry and then drop in blueberries.

Snowman

- 2 or 3 lettuce leaves
- 1 piece nori
- 2 rice balls (page 131), one bigger than the other
- 1 slice baby carrot
- 1 olive
- 1 piece sliced ham

1. Line the bento box with lettuce. Cut eyes and a smile out of nori and apply to the small rice ball. Cut a small piece of the baby carrot with a pinched straw for the snowman's nose.

2. Cut the black olive into small slices; punch out three buttons with a small drinking straw. Add them to the large rice ball. Cut a strip of ham and arrange like a scarf.

Fried Shrimp

- 2 or 3 large shrimp, cleaned and deveined
- 1 tbsp flour
- 1 egg, beaten
- 2 tbsp panko or regular bread crumbs
- several tbsp oil for frying

1. Leave shrimp tails attached. Make little cuts into the inner side to straighten them out.

2. Dredge shrimp in flour, dip in egg wash, and coat with panko or bread crumbs. Fry the shrimp on all sides until golden brown. Drain on a wire rack or paper towel. Cool completely.

> Pack a mini condiment container filled with tartar sauce or cocktail sauce for dipping shrimp.

Design your own bento and plan ahead in a bento diary or sketchbook!

As you shape the rice balls, you can fold in tasty morsels or fillings (pages 131 to 132).

It's important to eat a nutritious lunch on game day. Rice balls are healthy and filling, and they taste great with sliced kiwi, strawberries, and edamame or lima beans stacked onto food picks for easy nibbling. Just add a juice box and the game is on!

Sports Balls

- 1½ cups rice (page 130)
- a few tbsp ketchup
- pinch of salt
- 1 piece nori
- 2 lettuce leaves

1. Divide the rice into three portions. Mix ketchup into one portion until the rice is orange. Form one orange and two white balls using a mold or your hands. Stuff with the filling of your choice. Sprinkle with salt.

2. Cut thin strips of nori and wrap around the orange rice ball to resemble a basketball.

3. Cut pentagon shapes and thin, short strips out of nori for the soccer ball. Decorate the baseball with ketchup. Line the bento box with lettuce, add the rice balls, and fill the space around them with fruits and veggies.

Try making a football out of a beef cutlet (page 132) and white cheese, with a side of garlicky green beans (page 135).

Some mornings nothing seems to go right and time becomes an issue. A 4-in-1 sandwich cutter fits four different designs into one cutter and makes a homemade lunch quick and easy. Add carrot sticks, a sliced pickle, cheese cubes, and assorted fruit, and you're ready to go!

Smiling Sammies

- 2 slices bread
- 2 slices deli meat
- 1 or 2 slices cheese
- 1 piece nori

1. Use the sandwich cutter on the bread slices, cutting out the four designs. Continue cutting the deli meat and cheese slices. Assemble the sandwiches.

2. Use scissors or a punch to cut various smiley faces out of cheese or nori.

3. Line a sandwich box with lettuce leaves and place the sandwiches into the box, propping them up with carrot sticks as needed.

> **Individually packaged cheese is a yummy, healthful addition to any bento box.**

Cutting a sandwich into fun shapes with a sandwich cutter is as easy as 1, 2, 3.

Sunny-Side Up

Rainy days turn sunny-side up when there's a cheery egg-and-cheese omelet in your bento box!

An oval bento box is the perfect shape for a folded omelet. Fill the rest of the box with fresh herb and tomato salad, a scoop of pickled cabbage, and a bunch of red grapes. To get an early start, marinate the chicken the night before.

Omelet & Sunny Cheese Eggs

- 1 egg, beaten
- a few tsp extra-virgin olive oil
- 1 cup fillings, such as rice or pasta
- 1 slice white cheese
- ½ slice cheddar cheese
- 1 piece nori
- a dab of ketchup
- 1 sprig fresh parsley

1. Run the beaten egg through a strainer for a superfine color and texture. Warm oil in a pan over low heat and cook the omelet. Put omelet fillings on one side and fold it in half in the bento box.

2. Cut out two ovals from the white cheese and two smaller circles from the cheddar cheese. Put onto the omelet and microwave a few seconds. Punch out two nori faces and place on the "yolks." Use a toothpick to dab on rosy ketchup cheeks.

3. Cut out raindrops from the leftover cheddar cheese and add nori faces. Garnish with parsley.

Grilled Chicken

- 2 tsp soy sauce
- 1 tsp balsamic vinegar
- 3 or 4 bite-size pieces of chicken
- 2 lettuce leaves

1. Combine the soy sauce and vinegar in a zip-top plastic bag; add the chicken and let it marinate 30 minutes. When ready to cook, spit the chicken pieces on a skewer and broil in the oven or toaster oven until cooked. Line the open space in the bento box with lettuce leaves. Arrange chicken in the box.

Fresh Herb & Tomato Salad

- ½ small tomato
- 2 edamame pods
- 1 basil leaf, minced
- 1 tsp extra-virgin olive oil
- pinch of salt and pepper

1. Cut the tomato into quarters and remove the seeds. Shell the edamame pods. Combine all ingredients and mix well. Add to the bento box, using a food cup if needed.

Pickled Cabbage

- 2½ tbsp white vinegar
- 2 tbsp sugar
- 1 tsp oil
- 1 small handful shredded cabbage
- pinch of salt and pepper

1. Combine vinegar, sugar, and oil and bring to a boil until sugar dissolves.

2. Add cabbage and simmer about 1 minute over low heat. Drain and refrigerate. When cooled, add to the bento box with salt and pepper.

Additional Recipes for Mini Snacks and Save-It-for-Later Lunches

Cooking Rice

Cooking this healthy, filling food is quick and easy; it can be done either in a rice cooker or on the stove with an ordinary pot or pressure cooker. For rice balls, cook Japanese-style white rice, also known as high glutenous rice, japonica rice, sushi rice, or sticky rice. First, wash the uncooked rice thoroughly: In a pot or colander, cover rice with cold water, swish until water turns cloudy, and drain; repeat until water runs clear.

Stick with a 1 to 1⅓ or 1½ ratio of rice to water, such as 1 cup uncooked rice to 1½ cups water.

On the stove: Put washed rice into a pot or pressure cooker, add cold water, and bring to a full boil. Stir once or twice to prevent rice from sticking. Then tightly cover and reduce heat to low for 8 minutes. Turn off heat and keep covered to let steam 15 minutes, or until most of the water has evaporated.

In a rice cooker: Put washed rice into the cooker, add cold water, and press the "cook" button. High-tech rice warmers have specific functions and measurements for different types of rice, so be sure to read the manual carefully.

Keep the lid on no matter how eager you are to take a peek! Trapped steam makes rice fluffy and delicious.

Coloring Rice

Colored rice is an easy way to add a burst of color to your bento and create charaben in familiar colors. You can simply cook the rice in water tinted with food coloring, or you can stir in coloring, herbs, or spices after the rice is cooked. When adding color to cooked rice, make sure the rice is still hot. (Cold rice clumps together and does not mix well, leaving uneven spots of color.)

To color rice that's been frozen, microwave rice with a damp paper towel or add a sprinkling of water to it and seal the bowl with plastic wrap. Stir in coloring or spices once the rice is hot and fluffy.

red Hawaiian shrimp powder (*hana ebi*) red food coloring paprika red-pepper flakes Old Bay seasoning	dried parsley green food coloring minced broccoli spinach powder green Hawaiian shrimp powder (*hana ebi*)
red food coloring water left over from cooking red cabbage or beets plum vinegar powder (*hana osushi no moto*)	blue food coloring purple potato powder
	mashed purple sweet potato purple food coloring a mixture of red and blue food coloring purple potato powder
finely grated carrot red or yellow food coloring ketchup	soy sauce bonito flakes brown rice rice seasoning (*furikake*)
boiled egg yolk (crumbled or sliced) curry powder turmeric mashed squash yellow food coloring	ground black sesame seeds black food coloring

How to Make Rice Balls (*Onigiri*)

Our mothers took a splash of water, a pinch of salt, and a bit of rice in their hands, quickly seasoning and shaping rice at once. Today, it's common to use this easy plastic-wrap method to make tidy little balls of rice.

Unlike sushi rice, which is flavored with sugar and vinegar, onigiri rice is lightly salted and can be flavored or filled.

❶ You'll need plastic wrap, a scoop (about ⅓ cup) warm cooked rice, a rice paddle or large spoon, a tasty filling (optional), a few pinches of salt, and a piece of nori.

❷ Sprinkle salt into rice.

❸ Mix with a rice paddle, tossing to cool.

❹ Scoop rice onto plastic wrap. Make an indentation for a filling (if desired).

❺ Wrap rice with plastic wrap, shaping it into a triangle, ball, oval, or other shape.

❻ Plastic wrap helps shape rice and keeps it from sticking to your hands!

❼ Wrap with nori (cut into squares or into cute shapes with scissors or craft punches). If necessary, a dab of water will help it stick to rice.

❽ Serve traditionally with pickled bamboo shoots and a cup of tea.

Called *onigiri* in Japan and *musubi* in Hawaii, little handheld balls of rice are the perfect portable snack!

Filling Rice Balls

Try mixing herbs, spices, and diced meat or veggies into the rice before shaping it, or fold a spoonful of something yummy into the center of each ball. Traditionally, preservative fillings were preferred, such as salted salmon, Japanese pickled plums, kombu kelp seaweed, salted cod roe (*tarako*), bonito flakes (*katsuoboshi*), and other sour or salty foods. Today some of the most popular fillings include:

- baked salmon
- beef, chicken or pork cutlet
- bonito flakes with soy sauce
- chicken karaage, Japanese-style fried chicken
- diced shrimp with mayo
- fish roe or salmon caviar
- fried chicken
- green peas
- grilled salmon, chicken, beef, or SPAM
- kimchi
- Korean BBQ beef
- kombu kelp seaweed
- nori paste, ume paste, or sweet red bean paste (*anko*)
- pickled plums ("pickled ume," *umeboshi*)
- pickled vegetables
- scrambled egg
- shrimp or veggie tempura
- tuna with mayo

Tasty seasoned meat (*sato shayu*): 1 part soy sauce, 1 part sugar, 1 part mirin or water. Simmer meat in sauce 10 minutes, and then let cool before folding into a rice ball.

Sushi vinegar (*sushi su*): In a saucepan, combine ¼ cup rice vinegar, 2 tbsp sugar, ½ tsp grated ginger, and 1 tbsp mirin or cooking wine. Stir over medium heat until sugar is dissolved. Cool a few minutes; stir into the hot rice.

Mix sushi vinegar into rice to make sushi rice.

Fried Rice

Heat about 2 tbsp oil in a pan. Fry about 1 cup cooked rice with 2 tsp ketchup or 2 tsp soy sauce, salt, and pepper, stirring to distribute the color. While it's frying, you can crack an egg into it or mix in chopped meat or veggies; stir to distribute.

For Hawaiian-style fried rice: Add 2 tsp mirin with the ketchup or soy sauce.

Fried Rice Balls

Rice balls can be grilled, fried, or deep-fried until golden brown and crispy crunchy. Heat a few tsp oil in a pan. Brush rice balls with soy sauce and sprinkle with white sesame seeds. Grill a few minutes per side or until the surface is brown and crisp.

Main Dishes

Beef Cutlets
Makes about 5 servings, enough for leftovers

1 lb top sirloin, thinly sliced
salt and pepper
2 tbsp flour
3 eggs, beaten
1 cup bread crumbs
a few tsp oil

Season beef with salt and pepper. Dredge in flour, dip in egg wash, and coat in bread crumbs. Heat oil in a pan over medium-high heat. Fry the cutlets until browned on both sides.

Use this method to make quick chicken or pork cutlets!

Creamed Tuna
Makes about 4 servings, enough for leftovers

1 tbsp olive oil
1 small onion, chopped
1 can tuna, drained

1 can cream of mushroom soup
1 cup frozen peas
1 bag plain potato chips

Heat olive oil in a pan on medium heat and sauté onions 1 minute. Add tuna and combine well, flaking the fish. Mix in soup and peas. Crush the potato chips and add enough to cover the entire tuna mixture. Cover and simmer 5 to 10 minutes.

Green Pea Mac & Cheese
Makes 8 servings

Green peas make this classic dish nutritious—and pretty! Melt half a stick of butter in a saucepan over low heat. Add 2 or 3 tbsp flour to thicken. Pour in 1 can heavy cream and simmer, stirring occasionally. Boil 1 package of macaroni noodles 2 to 3 minutes; drain well. While the noodles are still hot, stir in cheese, about ½ cup cooked green peas, and creamy sauce.

Pressed for time? Stir frozen peas into a mac & cheese singles packet!

■ Green pea mac & cheese

Japanese-Style Fried Chicken (*Chicken Karaage*)
Makes about 6 servings, enough for leftovers

1½ lb skinless, boneless chicken thighs
2 eggs, lightly beaten
½ tsp salt
½ tsp black pepper
1 tbsp garlic, minced
1 tsp fresh ginger root, grated
1 tbsp sesame oil
1 tbsp sesame seeds
1 tbsp soy sauce
3 tbsp potato starch or cornstarch
1 tbsp rice flour
oil for frying

1. Remove the fat from the chicken thighs and cut into bite-size pieces.

2. In a large bowl, combine eggs, salt, pepper, garlic, ginger, sesame oil, sesame seeds, and soy sauce. Add chicken pieces and mix well. Cover and marinate in fridge 30 minutes.

3. Add potato starch and rice flour to a zip-top plastic bag. Place chicken in the bag, close, and shake to coat.

4. Fry in oil in a pan or a deep fryer until golden brown. Cool on a wire rack or paper towel.

Korean BBQ Beef
Makes about 6 servings, enough to share!

1 cup sugar
1 cup water
1 cup soy sauce
½ medium onion, grated
2 tbsp minced garlic
2 tbsp sesame oil
1 tbsp pepper

continued from page 133

1 tbsp grated ginger
1 lb flank steak

1. Combine sugar, water, soy sauce, onion, garlic, sesame oil, pepper, and ginger in a zip-top plastic bag. Slice the flank steak into thin strips, cross-cut. Add meat to the bag and marinate 30 minutes.

2. Fry the meat in a pan over medium-high heat until cooked through and slightly burned; alternatively, grill until cooked through.

Pan-Seared Salmon

1 salmon fillet, cut into bite-size pieces
½ tbsp lemon juice
½ tbsp extra-virgin olive oil
pinch of salt

1. Place salmon in a plastic zip-top bag with lemon juice, olive oil, and salt. Seal the bag and toss to coat; let rest 15 minutes. In a lightly oiled pan over medium-high heat, sear salmon 2 minutes.

2. Reduce to medium heat and cover until salmon is fully cooked, about 4 minutes.

Side Dishes

Cheesy Sausage

Cut a breakfast sausage or ½ hot dog in half lengthwise. Sandwich a slice of cheese and sauté 1 minute or until the cheese starts to melt. Stick a decorative food pick down the center to make it finger food.

■ Cheesy sausage

Crêpe-Style Omelet (*Usuyaki Tamago*)

Beat 1 egg yolk. Add a dash of salt and pour egg yolk through a tea strainer for extra-smooth color and texture. Warm oil in a pan over low heat. Pour the yolk into the pan and cook until just set.

■ Crêpe-style omelet

Fried Tofu

Drain thinly sliced tofu by putting it under a weight (such as a heavy pan) for about 6 hours. Press with a paper towel to dry. Deep fry the tofu 8 minutes at 240°F, take it out of the oil for a few minutes, and then fry it again at 375°F until golden brown.

For fried tofu skins: Pat with a paper towel to remove excess oil. Combine ¾ cup water with

1 tbsp soy sauce, 1 tbsp sugar, and 1 tbsp sake in a saucepan; bring to a boil. Add the tofu and simmer 15 minutes over low heat. Remove tofu and squeeze it in a paper towel to dry.

Thinly sliced tofu, called fried tofu skins or aburaage, can be store-bought or homemade with this recipe. They make yummy pockets for other foods!

■ Meat-wrapped okra

■ Meat-wrapped green beans

■ Fried tofu   ■ Fried tofu skin

Garlicky Green Beans

Heat 1 tsp extra-virgin olive oil in a pan over medium heat. Add 1 clove minced garlic. Sauté 5 or 6 green beans until they start to turn bright green. Mix 2 tbsp water with ½ tsp chicken bouillon and a pinch of salt and pepper; add to beans, cover, and simmer about 5 minutes. Uncover and cook until the liquid evaporates.

Meat-Wrapped Veggies

You can make this yummy finger food by wrapping cooked veggies (such as green beans, asparagus, mushrooms, or cauliflower) with strips of uncooked meat (such as bacon, ham, salami, or prosciutto). Wrap them with meat, securing the end with a toothpick. Brown on all sides in a pan, sealing the meat around the veggies. Remove toothpick and add to the bento box.

Mozzarella Tomatoes

Cut 2 cherry tomatoes in half; insert a small piece of fresh mozzarella cheese. Sandwich tomatoes back together with food picks or toothpicks. Mozzarella tomatoes are great for filling gaps in your bento box.

Pickled Sweet-and-Sour Tomatoes

Tangy sweet pickled tomatoes make it easy to eat your veggies! Remove stems from 6 or 7 cherry or grape tomatoes. Boil 10 seconds. Gently peel off the skins and put them in a jar. Bring 2⅔ tbsp vinegar, 1 tbsp sugar, 5½ tbsp water, and a pinch of salt and pepper to a boil in a saucepan. Stir until the sugar dissolves. Let sweet-and-sour vinegar syrup cool and then pour it over the tomatoes. Let stand 6 to 8 hours. Garnish with a sprinkling of olive oil and fresh basil.

■ Pickled sweet-and-sour tomatoes

Rolled-Up Omelet (*Tamagoyaki*)

Pack bite-size protein into a lunch with this classic Japanese snack, known as tamagoyaki or "Japanese egg roll." It couldn't be easier to make! Beat 1 or 2 eggs with a pinch of salt and chopped scallions or other mix-ins. Fry in a pan over low heat, letting the batter spread thinly. Once cooked through, cut the omelet in half, fold it into a tidy roll, and slice it into 1-inch pieces. Skewer each with a food pick.

These mini rolled-up omelets can be made ahead of time and refrigerated!

■ Rolled-up omelet

Salty-Sweet Spinach

Freshly cooked spinach can be delicious; it isn't just for Popeye anymore. Heat 2 tsp extra-virgin olive oil in a pan. Add 2 or 3 handfuls of spinach leaves, 1 tsp soy sauce, and 1 tsp sugar, stirring until almost wilted. Sprinkle with ½ tsp ground white sesame seeds and ½ tsp white sesame seeds and a pinch of coarse salt.

You can substitute soy sauce, sugar, and sesame seeds with 1 clove diced garlic and a pinch of red pepper flakes. Experiment with your favorite spices!

For cooked spinach: Try the recipe on page 27. Or boil 1 oz fresh spinach for 30 seconds. Drain and cut spinach into bite-size pieces. Mix in ½ tsp soy sauce and 1 tbsp dried bonito flakes or other seasonings.

Simmered Squash or Pumpkin

Use this recipe to make any pumpkin or squash extra tasty! Wash it and remove tough skin and pulp. A potato peeler can cut decorative stripes into the skin. Slice into 2-inch cubes. Put them into a saucepan with 1 cup broth (chicken, vegetable, or dashi), about 3 tbsp sugar, and 1 tbsp soy sauce. Bring to a boil and lower the heat, simmering 10 minutes or until tender.

Mixed veggies simmered in a seasoned broth won in a poll asking Japanese women what they most loved to cook for their families.

Tuna-Fish Salad

Combine 1 can drained tuna fish, 2 tbsp mayo, 2 grated mini carrots, and a pinch of salt. Scoop it into the box. Add a food divider or wax paper to keep it separated from the other foods.

Eat your veggies! Try mixing in finely chopped parsley or finely chopped carrots, celery, or other veggies. You can make tuna-fish salad even healthier by replacing the mayo with extra-virgin olive oil.

Sauces, Dips, and Salad Dressings

Simple Vinaigrette

Slowly add 3 parts extra-virgin olive oil to 1 part rice or wine vinegar plus lemon juice, whisking until combined. Herbs, spices, salt, and pepper can be added to taste.

Somen Sauce
This super-delicious sauce for somen (Japanese noodles) comes from Pikko's mom. Combine 1 cup shoyu, 1 cup sugar, 2 tbsp sesame oil, and a pinch of ground sesame seeds. Stir vigorously and pour over cooked and chilled somen noodles.

Soy Mayo
Soy Mayo tastes great as a dip or dressing for veggies such as steamed asparagus and green beans. Mix 1 tbsp mayonnaise with 1 tsp soy sauce and stir to combine. Add ½ tsp black sesame.

Or try ketchup mayo: Mix 1 tbsp mayonnaise with ketchup to taste.

Tonkatsu Sauce
It's easy to make this tasty sauce for tonkatsu (pork cutlets). Mix 3 tbsp ketchup with 1 tsp dark soy sauce or Worcestershire sauce.

Veggie Dip
Combine 1 cup low-fat plain yogurt, 1 tbsp minced celery, 1 tbsp minced onion, 1 tsp lemon juice, and 1 tsp salt.

Desserts

Jell-O Snacks
Colorful, jiggly gelatin is perfect for bento boxes. You can cut it into shapes with cookie cutters or mold it into fun shapes with little silicone molds. Use food cups, dividers, or cupcake cups to keep your Jell-O treats separate from other foods.

Pretty Pink Mini Cupcakes
Line a mini cupcake pan with mini cupcake wrappers. Fill with a cake box mix and bake according to package instructions. Stir several drops of neon pink food coloring into a basic homemade buttercream or store-bought frosting. Top with sprinkles!

■ Pretty pink mini-cupcakes

Wrapped Candies
Prettily wrapped candies are a sweet addition to any bento box.

You can twist colorful cellophane around any home-made treat, such as nibble-size fudge squares, mini cookies, or little caramel-corn balls.

How to Make a Hatching Chick

Hatching chicks are a cute addition to Easter baskets or any bento box.

Cheep, cheep!

❶ You'll need 1 hard-boiled egg, 1 piece of salami (or thinly sliced carrot), 1 piece of nori, a hole punch, and a sharp, pointy knife.

❷ Start the zigzag cut with the tip of the knife.

❸ Continue around the egg, slightly lifting the top occasionally to check that you aren't cutting too far into the yolk.

❹ Gently remove the top of the egg white. Use a hole punch to make two eyes out of nori.

❺ Cut a triangle beak out of salami (or carrot).

❻ Apply the eyes and beak with tweezers. A dab of moisture will help them stick.

Shopping Guide

All the bento box materials you need are as close as your local grocery or craft store. But it's always fun to explore the wide world of bento tools and accessories. You may find the following suppliers useful in your bento-making adventures.

Amazon (*www.amazon.com*): Third-party sellers have lots of bento boxes for sale, and Amazon has an endless supply of cookie cutters, fondant cutters, thermal lunch jars, and of course cookbooks. Shop their Grocery section for Asian foods!

Bake It Pretty (*www.bakeitpretty.com*): This online shop stocks lovely baking products and kitchen kits, as well as cupcake tools and decorations in hard-to-find designs and colors.

Bento & Co (*www.bentoandco.com*): Based in Japan, this online shop sells a variety of beautiful, high-end bento boxes and cute accessories. The site is in French and currency is in Euros.

Bento Crazy (*www.bentocrazy.ecrater.com*): Based in Maryland, this store specializes in everything bento, from boxes to sauce bottles to oshibori.

Candyland Crafts (*www.candylandcrafts.com*): Candy and cupcake supplies.

Daiso Japan (*www.daisojapan.com*): Daiso sells bento boxes and a few accessories in bulk, so it's a great place to shop if you're planning on making bento goodie bags for a party.

Design Within Reach (*www.dwr.com*): Dedicated to simple, elegant design solutions, DWR carries some bento-making items, such as handy kitchen tools and colorful Japanese masking tapes.

Dunwoody Booth Packaging (*www.dunwoody-booth.com*): Boxes, tins, ribbon, accessories.

eBay (*www.ebay.com*): eBay is a great place to find bento boxes and accessories as well as unusual cutters, molds, and craft tools perfect for making creative bento boxes.

Etsy Shops (*www.etsy.com*): Individual sellers provide an endless selection of bento boxes, tools, accessories—and even bento-themed jewelry

From Japan with Love (*www.fromjapanwithlove.com*): A Yahoo! Store run by a couple in Japan, they sell lots of items not found anywhere else online, such as sandwich cutters and nori punches.

Happy Japan (*www.happyjapan.net*): An online store with a physical shop in Tennessee, Happy Japan carries a wide assortment of bento boxes and accessories.

Happy Tiffin (*www.happytiffin.com*): Specializing in stainless steel tiffins, lunch containers that are great for packing your bento. They offer single-tier tiffins or sets with up to four tiers.

I Love Obento! (*www.iloveobento.com*): One of the few places online to get Carl Craft punches, this store also carries lots of fun bento accessories and boxes.

J-List/J-Box (*www.jbox.com*): This Japan/San Diego–based company always has oodles of bento goodies for sale. Join their affiliate program so you can start earning money for free products!

Japan Centre (*www.japancentre.com*): Based in London, this online Japanese culinary shop stocks all sorts of handpicked Japanese foods, beverages, bento boxes, and cookware. Ships to the United Kingdom, Europe, and beyond.

Kitchen Krafts (*www.kitchenkrafts.com*): Known as the "foodcrafter's supply catalog," Kitchen Krafts stocks home baking supplies including many products perfect for bento-making, such as fondant cutters, mini cookie cutters, and cupcake accessories.

Laptop Lunches (*www.laptoplunches.com*): Based in California, Laptop Lunches promotes healthful eating and waste reduction via practical, reusable food containers and "bento-ware for everywhere."

Life Without Plastic (*www.lifewithoutplastic.com*): Dedicated to a greener planet, this store offers a variety of wood and metal bento boxes to help decrease the world's dependence on plastic.

Marukai (*www.marukaiestore.com*): The online store for Marukai, a Japanese market, their boxes are pricey, but they carry some bento accessories for bargain prices. This is a great place to shop for Japanese foods and sauces.

Michaels Craft Stores (*www.michaels.com*): Craft stores like Michaels and Jo-Ann Fabrics are great places to pick up affordable supplies like silicone molds, colored tape, and scrapbooking punches for bento use.

Rakuten International (*en.rakuten.co.jp*): This online shopping mall is like a Japanese Amazon. It sells a wide variety of Japanese products, including bento boxes, tools, and accessories, and ships to most locations worldwide.

Sugar Charms (*www.sugarcharms.com*): A store for all things cute, Sugar Charms has a large selection of bento boxes, onigiri cases, and bags.

Tupperware (*www.order.tupperware.com*): Sealable plastic containers are a good alternative or supplement to classic bento boxes. Individual containers for baby food work well for small snacks and freezing prepared foods for later use.

Urban Outfitters (*www.urbanoutfitters.com*): Urban Outfitters, Anthropologie, and other retail stores often carry creative cookware, American-style lunchboxes, and bento boxes.

Williams-Sonoma (*www.williams-sonoma.com*): Culinary stores like Williams-Sonoma and Sur La Table stock a wide variety of containers, tools, and gadgets perfect for bento making: mini cookie cutters and pie cutters, themed silicone molds, individually portioned containers, kitchen scissors, and much more.

Glossary

Here's a list of common Japanese and Hawaiian bento terms.

aburaage: fried tofu skin

croquette: a small fried food roll usually containing as main ingredients mashed potatoes and/or minced meat fried in bread crumbs

dashi: a Japanese soup stock made from seaweed or fish

dashimaki tamago: Japanese rolled egg flavored with dashi

donburi: a dish served over rice in a bowl

ebi fry: shrimp fried in a panko batter

edamame: soy beans

furikake: rice seasoning, comes packaged in a variety of flavors

hana ebi: Red Hawaiian shrimp powder

hana osushi no moto: plum vinegar powder, used as seasoning and natural pink food coloring

haupia: coconut pudding

inarizushi: simmered aburaage, used for sushi

kanikama: imitation crab stick

katsu: breaded, fried meat rolls; similar to croquettes

karaage: Japanese-style fried chicken

katsuobushi: dried flaked fish seasoning, also called bonito flakes

loco moco: Hawaiian dish consisting of a hamburger patty on hot rice topped with a fried egg and gravy

lomilomi salmon: a salted salmon, tomato, onion, and green onion salad, served cold

makizushi: sushi roll wrapped in nori

memmi sauce: noodle soup base (*mentsuyu* in Japan) and dipping sauce

mirin: sweet rice wine; substitute with any cooking wine, dry sherry, sweet marsala, or sweet white wine.

mochiko flour: sweet rice flour

musubi: onigiri (rice ball) wrapped in nori

nikumaki: vegetables wrapped in chicken and fried

nori: seaweed paper

onigiri: rice ball

panko: Japanese-style bread crumbs (now sold by Progresso)

ponzu sauce: Japanese sauce made with mirin, rice vinegar, katsuobushi flakes, seaweed, and citrus

rice vinegar: vinegar made from fermented rice

roasted sesame: roasted sesame seeds

sake: rice wine

sato shoyu: a sauce made from soy sauce and sugar

shiitake mushroom: a Japanese variety of mushroom

shimeji mushroom: an East Asian mushroom

soboro: a minced or crumbled meat or egg dish

somen: thin, white wheat noodle

soy paper: alternative to nori, available in a variety of bright colors

sushi su: used to flavor sushi rice

tamagoyaki: Japanese rolled egg

tamari soy sauce: gluten-free dark soy sauce

tarako: salted cod roe

tempura: shrimp or vegetables fried in a light batter and dipped in sauce

tonkatsu: fried pork cutlets, a type of katsu

umeboshi: pickled plums

usuyaki tamago: bright yellow Japanese crêpe-style omelet

wasabi: horseradish paste

Metric Conversion Chart

Volume

U.S.	Metric
¼ tsp	1.25 ml (cc)
½ tsp	2.5 ml (cc)
1 tsp	5 ml (cc)
1 tbsp (3 tsp)	15 ml (cc)
1 fl oz (2 tbsp)	30 ml (cc)
¼ cup	60 ml (cc)
⅓ cup	80 ml (cc)
½ cup	120 ml (cc)
1 cup	240 ml (cc)
1 pint (2 cups)	480 ml (cc)
1 quart (2 pints)	960 ml (cc)
1 gallon (4 quarts)	3.84 liters

❁ Japanese bento makers typically use cubic centimeter (cc) measurements. Use this conversion chart to share bento recipes with friends worldwide.

Weight

U.S.	Metric
1 oz	28 g
4 oz (¼ lb)	113 g
8 oz (½ lb)	227 g
12 oz (¾ lb)	340 g
16 oz (1 lb)	454 g
2.2 lb	1 kg

Length

Inches	Centimeters
¼	0.65
½	1.25
1	2.50
2	5.00
3	7.50
4	10.0
5	12.5
6	15.0

Oven Temperature

Degrees Fahrenheit	Degrees Centigrade	British Gas Marks
200	93	—
250	120	½
275	140	1
300	150	2
325	165	3
350	175	4
375	190	5
400	200	6
450	230	8

Acknowledgments

Heartfelt thanks to my mother-in-law, June Watanabe, for her wonderful meals that feed me, my family, and my blog. To my mother, thank you for sharing your secret recipes with me. To Grandma Mu, thank you for showing me the value of simple comfort foods. Love to my husband Randall and my kids for being supportive and letting me take over our kitchen with my obsession. Big thanks to Michael Burke for the mochiko chicken recipe and to my cousin Jennifer Webster for the constant advice, laughs, and mac & cheese recipe. To Margaret, Jenny, and the staff at Quirk, thank you from the bottom of my heart for making a dream come true. You've been a phenomenal group to work with and ever so patient with my endless questions and suggestions!

—Pikko

I want to say thank you to my children, Kai and Hal, for being my #1 fans, and to my husband, Yo, for watching affectionately as my bento work progressed. To my friends, who are all looking forward to this book, thank you so much for all the support you've given me. Many thanks to the kind and helpful folks at Quirk Books.

—Maki

Thank you, friends! We hope that our cute, yummy bento will bring smiles to many faces.

irreference \ir-'ef-(ə-)rən(t)s\ n (2009)

1 : irreverent reference
2 : real information that also entertains or amuses

How-Tos. Quizzes. Instructions.
Recipes. Crafts. Jokes.
Trivia. Games. Tricks.
Quotes. Advice. Tips.

Learn something. Or not.

VISIT IRREFERENCE.COM
The New Quirk Books Web Site